# FOOD
# WEIGHTS and MEASURES

*A Reference Tool for Product Development*

*Recipe Costing and Nutrient Analyses*

## MA. CHRISTINA G. AQUINO
## JANINE P. SIGGAOAT

TABULA RASA CONSULTING CORP.

Manila

First Printing, 2015

ISBN 978-1507609804

1601 Block 16 Eagle Avenue, Camella Alabang 2
Muntinlupa City 1770, Metro Manila, Philippines
E-mail: trcc4613@gmail.com

Cover photography by SelfPubBookCovers.com/Chthonika

# Acknowledgements

The authors would like to say a heartfelt appreciation to the following organizations and people who have made this project possible.

- To *Lyceum of the Philippines University Manila* for the use of Food Laboratory and Kitchen.
- To *United States Department of Agriculture, Agricultural Research Service* for allowing us to use the nutrient database for standard reference.
- To *www.pixabay.com* for the free sharing of photographs. Special thanks for the following photographers and contributors: Hans, Simon, Weinstock, Nemo, Openclips and Public Domain pictures.
- To *family and friends* who provide emotional support for the researchers, especially for the family time that given in the project.
- To *Jose R. del Fierro* for sharing in part of the development fee of this project.

This page intentionally left blank.

*To our loving and faithful*
*ALMIGHTY GOD*

.

This page intentionally left blank.

# Contents

This page intentionally left blank.

# INTRODUCTION

*Abraham Maslow's Theory of Hierarchy of Needs* identifies several needs and that some needs take precedence over others. One of the needs is physiological needs that include food, shelter and clothing. Because of its basic characteristic, food places the highest attention and cut across social status and gender issues.

Food may come from various sources. Whether preparing food in small or large quantities the need for the use of measures is essential. This guarantees consistent products and yields a standardized combination of flavors, textures and nutrient values.

Weight measures are more accurate than volume measures. Food ingredients' packaging uses weight measures in metric. It's easier to cost if the weights of volume measures basing on the fractions of the packaged details in the weight and cost of ingredients. Translating a recipe that yields 6 to 100 servings simplifies better if the volume measures are in weights. With rising costs of ingredients and the need to ensure that every penny counts, homemakers, entrepreneurs and even manufacturing companies put much importance on the costs of ingredients. A daunting task to achieve a goal of balancing a satisfying, and quality meal yet cost-effective.

Government in most countries regulates that all food products sold in the public has information on the labels. Laws include the use of metric. The base units of weight and volume are grams and liters respectively. With this, homemakers and entrepreneurs cuts outguesses on how to control food costs. Also, this reduces overestimation or underestimation when buying ingredients; therefore prevents food waste.

An assessment of individual diet or a population entails use of food weights in grams as all data on food composition are in 100 grams basis. Readily information on food weights and measures basing on metric aid health professionals, dietitians, nutrition education experts, agriculturists, economist, and policy-makers oversee an individual nutritional status. It also covers surveying of malnutrition cases nationally for those who are micronutrient deficient, underweight and obese that yields to developing intervention programs and food-based dietary guidelines.

The basic assumption of converting 1 teaspoon to 5 grams as "*standard*" is perhaps because of the absence of information or confusion in volume and weight measures. There can't be any standard weight for a cup of different ingredients because of the variances in mass, density, specifications of ingredients. Like sugar has many market forms; *demerara, muscovado, brown, white, caster* or *powdered*. There are obvious physical differences and to say simply that a cup of sugar weighs 240 grams will be a great error. Besides, foods as biological materials show natural variations. This variability widens by different planting, harvesting, storage and transport practices. Processed foods often changes in formula and production.

This book provides an estimate weight of Asian ingredients using the household measure of one cup. The values set in the list regards as "*best estimates*" not an "*absolute value.*" The list includes cereals, fruits, vegetables, legumes, nuts, seeds, meats, fishes, dairy, eggs, fats and oils and other commonly used ingredients. However, data contained on the list are far from complete. Considering the ever-increasing number of new food preparation and made products introduced continuously, it is therefore, unlikely to cover them all at once. Priorities are first set covering the most common ingredients available in the market. Adding other records of items is due in the future publications.

Containing 500 plus ingredients surveyed spreading to 2000 and more weights and measures recorded. This is a valuable tool for professionals in the food service industry and public health nutrition. Data produced gives a useful means in standardizing recipes, costing and quantifying as well evaluating nutrient quality of meals.

# Methodology

## *Sampling*

Assigning priorities for inclusion in this list are from cookbooks, and from food items recorded in the Philippine Food Composition Tables 1990. Food samples are from public markets of Cartimar and Libertad in Pasay City, Philippines as well in Quiapo and Divisoria Market in Manila, Philippines. Also, in high-end supermarkets of SM Makati, Rustan's, Cash-and-Carry in Makati City, Philippines. For processed ingredients, taking 1 kilogram for each sample with at least three to four brands while getting 500 grams in each market are sampling procedures for fresh, raw ingredients. Keeping the quality of the food samples throughout the experiment is a basic consideration to lessen any moisture gain or losses of the food samples.

## *Instruments Used*

Using a digital weighing scale that registers a maximum of 5000 grams to a minimum of 1 gram measures the weight of the food samples. The researcher calibrates the scale each food sample weighing following good laboratory practices. Weighing the food samples three times with different cups yields average weights of the food sample.

## *Sample Preparation*

For preparing the food samples, the following is the guides:
(1) Writing the descriptions about part, maturity, variety, color, shape, packing medium and manner of preparation;
(2) Draining well all bottled or canned products before pooling or mixing with other brands;
(3) Packing firmly or loosely and leveling to the rim of the standard measuring cups. Packing of the three measuring cups before weighing.
(4) Removing the nonedible portions of the raw ingredients.
(5) Slicing suitable cuts like dice, strips, rounds, mince, and grate.
(6) Applying different cooking methods suited to the food samples.
(7) Cooling cooked food samples before weighing.

### *Food Sample Measurements*

Weighing liquid samples like milk, sauces, oils, syrups, molasses and fluid-type solids like applesauce, ketchup and mayonnaise take the volumetric glassware using the direct fill technique. Transferring the food samples carefully to Pyrex glass measuring cup, and allowing time for settling because viscous liquids are higher in the center when first poured. Readings are at the lowest part of the meniscus and avoiding to make parallax error. If the food sample reaches the line for one cup, taking the weights of the cup follows. For weighing clear liquids, putting a dark material behind the meniscus improve the observation.

For fine particulate solids like flour, measuring its weight comes in two ways: stirring or unstirring and spooning or dipping. For weighing medium particulate solids like chopped nuts, fruits, or dried pastas follow the step of filling the cup correctly. The volume above the fill line nearly equal to the free airspace between particles immediately below the fill line. It is leveled off with a metal spatula to have a flat surface before weighing.

### *Unavailability of Food Samples*

There are ingredients unavailable during gathering of food samples either due that it's not harvest time or peak season; or goods are out-of-stock. From here, the list borrows data from the *United States Department of Agriculture National Nutrient Database for Standard Reference, Release 27.*

# Guides in Using the Book

There are terms which will help to understand the data in this book.

| WORD | DEFINITION |
| --- | --- |
| Baked | To cook in an oven |
| Boil | To cook rapidly in water or liquid so that bubbles rise and break on the surface |
| Braised | To cook in small amount of liquid at low heat for a period of time |
| Broiled | To cook food over or under the heat source. |
| Buying guides | This will include the following information: market units that reflect commonly available sizes in the retail outlets, approximate volume per market unit and approximate weight per cup |
| Chop | To cut food into small pieces with a knife or chopping equipment |
| Dice | To cut into cubes with a knife or cutting equipment<br>Small dice – ½ x ½ x ½ inch<br>Medium dice – ¾ x ¾ x ¾ inch<br>Large dice – 1 x 1 x 1 inch |
| Edible Portion (EP) | The part of the food product that can be eaten after trimming and removing non-edible components. |
| Firmly packed | With a spatula, the ingredient is pressed tightly as possible into the measuring device |
| Food | Any substance, whether processed, semi-processed or raw, intended for human consumption and includes chewing gum, drinks and beverages and any substance which has been used as an ingredient or a component in the manufacture, preparation or treatment of food. (Consumer Act of the Philippines) |
| Fry | To cook in a small amount of fat over heat in a skillet, pan or griddle |
| Grind | To pulverize food |
| Julienned | To cut into strips |

| WORD | DEFINITION |
|---|---|
| Level | A precise measure of an ingredient, discarding all of the ingredients that rises above the rim of the measuring cup. Sweeping across the top of the measure with the blade of a spatula |
| Loosely packed | The ingredients is pressed lightly into the measuring device, only tightly enough to ensure no air pockets |
| Mince | is a cooking technique in which food ingredients are finely divided. The effect is to create a closely bonded mixture of ingredients and a soft or pasty texture |
| Mix | To blend or combine two or more ingredients |
| Peel | To strip off the outer covering of a food |
| Philippine ingredients | These are ingredients that are commercially available in the market in the preparation of Philippine dishes |
| Quantification | This is converting a household recipe for yields of more than 25 servings or more. |
| Shred | To cut foods into narrow strips |
| Standard cup | The standard cup is the cup that is used for measuring dry ingredients and is equivalent to 16 tablespoons. |
| Sweetened | With nutritive carbohydrate sweeteners added |
| Unsweetened | Without the addition of nutritive carbohydrate sweeteners |
| Flavored | Flavor derived substantially from an added flavoring ingredient |
| Processed foods | foods have been altered from their natural state for safety reasons and for convenience. The methods used for processing foods include canning, freezing, refrigeration, dehydration and aseptic processing. |
| Raw foods | unprocessed foods that have not been heated above 115 degrees Fahrenheit (46 degrees Celsius |

## ABBREVIATION and SYMBOLS

| | |
|---|---|
| Cup | *c* |
| Fluid ounce | *fl oz* |
| Liter | *l* |
| Milliliter | *ml* |
| Pint | *pt* |
| Quart | *qt* |
| Tablespoon | *Tbsp* |
| Teaspoon | *tsp* |
| Centimeter | *cm* |
| Diameter | *diam* |
| Inch | *in* |
| Gram | *g* |
| Kilogram | *kg* |
| Pound | *lb* |

## WEIGHT and VOLUME EQUIVALENTS

| | |
|---|---|
| 1 gram | = 0.035 ounces |
| 1 kilogram | = 2.21 pounds |
| 1 ounce | = 28.35 grams |
| 1 pound | = 453.59 grams |
| | |
| 1 Tbsp | = 3 tsp |
| 1 c | = 16 Tbsp |
| 1 pint | = 2 c |
| 1 qt | = 2 pt |
| 1 gal | = 4 qt |
| 1 lb | = 16 oz |

This page intentionally left blank.

# CEREALS, ROOTS, TUBERS and PRODUCTS

# CEREALS, ROOTS, TUBERS and PRODUCTS

**ARROWROOT**

| | |
|---|---|
| 1 piece root, raw | = 33g |
| 1 cup, peeled, sliced, raw | = 132g |
| 1 cup, peeled, sliced, boiled | = 145g |
| 1 cup, flour, unstirred, spooned | = 130g |
| 1 cup, flour, stirred, spooned | = 104g |

**BARLEY**

| | |
|---|---|
| 1 cup, pearl, boiled | = 200g |
| 1 cup, pearl, uncooked | = 150g |
| 1 cup, flour, stirred, spooned | = 150g |

**BISCUITS**

| | |
|---|---|
| 1 cup, Hi-Ro, ground, firmly packed | = 155g |
| 1 cup, Graham, ground, firmly packed | = 129g |
| 1 cup, Graham, ground, loosely packed | = 112g |

**BREADCRUMBS**

| | |
|---|---|
| 1 cup, coarse, loosely packed | = 50g |
| 1 cup, fine, firmly packed | = 154g |
| 1 cup, fine, loosely packed | = 110g |

**BUCKWHEAT**

| | |
|---|---|
| 1 cup, groats, roasted, cooked | = 168g |
| 1 cup, groats, roasted, uncooked | = 164g |
| 1 cup, flour, stirred, spooned | = 120g |

**BULGUR**

| | |
|---|---|
| 1 cup, boiled | = 182g |
| 1 cup, uncooked | = 140g |
| 1 cup, flour, stirred, spooned | = 140g |
| 1 cup, flour, unstirred, spooned | = 129g |

# CEREALS, ROOTS, TUBERS and PRODUCTS

## CASSAVA

| | |
|---|---|
| 1 extra-small tuber, with skin, raw | =  85g |
| 1 small tuber, with skin, raw | = 125g |
| 1 medium tuber, with skin, raw | = 250g |
| 1 large tuber, with skin, raw | = 1000g |
| | |
| 1 cup, tuber, skinned, chopped, raw | = 165g |
| 1 cup, tuber, skinned, chopped, boiled | = 194g |
| 1 cup, skinned, boiled, mashed | = 248g |

## CORN

| | |
|---|---|
| 1 ear, *baby corn* | =  8g |
| 1 ear, small, white, 5 ½ inch to 6 ½ inch, raw | =  73g |
| 1 ear, medium, white, 6 ¾ inch to 7 ½ inch, raw | =  90g |
| 1 ear, large, white, 7 ¾ inch to 9 inch, raw | = 143g |
| | |
| 1 cup, *white*, whole kernel, raw | = 145g |
| 1 cup, *white*, whole kernel, boiled | = 149g |
| 1 cup, *yellow*, whole kernel, raw | = 154g |
| 1 cup, *yellow*, whole kernel, boiled | = 157g |
| 1 cup, *white*, whole kernel, sweet, canned, drained | = 164g |
| 1 cup, *yellow*, whole kernel, sweet, canned, drained | = 184g |
| | |
| 1 cup, *cornmeal*, white | = 122g |
| 1 cup, *cornmeal*, yellow | = 122g |
| 1 cup, *pop*, cooked | =  30g |
| 1 cup, *pop*, cooked, sweetened | =  24g |
| 1 cup, *pop*, uncooked | = 208g |
| | |
| 1 cup, *flour*, stirred, dipped | = 105g |
| 1 cup, *flour*, stirred, spooned | =  95g |
| 1 cup, *flour*, unstirred, spooned | = 103g |

# CEREALS, ROOTS, TUBERS and PRODUCTS

Figure 1. *Uncooked canton noodles*

# CEREALS, ROOTS, TUBERS and PRODUCTS

## COUSCOUS
| | |
|---|---|
| 1 cup, boiled | = 160g |
| 1 cup, uncooked | = 175g |

## CRACKER CHIPS
| | |
|---|---|
| 1 cup, dried, Prawn flavor | = 105g |
| 1 cup, deep-fried, Prawn flavor | = 10g |
| 1 cup, crumbed, Prawn flavor | = 20g |

## NOODLES
| | |
|---|---|
| 1 cup, *Chow Mien*, boiled | = 50g |
| 1 cup, *Canton*, uncooked | = 40g |
| 1 cup, *Canton*, boiled | = 160g |
| 1 cup, *Champon*, uncooked | = 100g |
| 1 cup, *Champon*, boiled | = 170g |
| 1 cup, *Miki*, uncooked | = 100g |
| 1 cup, *Miki*, boiled | = 159g |
| 1 cup, *Rice noodles* (*Palabok*), thick thread, boiled | = 131g |
| 1 cup, *Rice noodles* (*Palabok*), thin thread, boiled | = 129g |
| 1 cup, *Rice noodles* (*Bihon*), thin thread, raw | = 72g |
| 1 cup, *Rice noodles* (*Bihon*), thin thread, boiled | = 180g |
| 1 cup, *Rice noodles* (*Miswa*), thin thread, raw | = 35g |
| 1 cup, *Rice noodles* (*Miswa*), thin thread, boiled | = 142g |
| 1 cup, *Soba*, boiled | = 120g |
| 1 cup, *Somen,* boiled | = 175g |
| 1 cup, *Sotanghon,* boiled | = 140g |
| 1 cup, *Tonkutsu,* uncooked | = 75g |
| 1 cup, *Tonkutsu,* boiled | = 190g |
| 1 cup, *Tsukemen,* uncooked | = 60g |
| 1 cup, *Tsukumen,* boiled | = 145g |
| 1 cup, *Yakisoba,* uncooked | = 75g |
| 1 cup, *Yakisoba,* boiled | = 190g |

# CEREALS, ROOTS, TUBERS and PRODUCTS

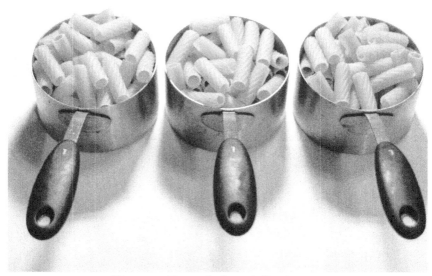

**Figure 2.** *Uncooked tortiglioni pasta*

**Figure 3.** *Cooked tortiglioni pasta*

# CEREALS, ROOTS, TUBERS and PRODUCTS

## OATS

| | |
|---|---|
| 1 cup, *oatbran*, boiled | = 230g |
| 1 cup, *oatbran*, uncooked | = 100g |
| 1 cup, *rolled*, loosely packed | = 100g |
| 1 cup, *rolled*, firmly packed | = 120g |
| 1 cup, *flour*, stirred, spooned | = 110g |

## PASTA

| | |
|---|---|
| 1 cup, *bowties*, boiled | = 123g |
| 1 cup, *bowties*, uncooked | = 76g |
| 1 cup, *cappelleti*, boiled | = 111g |
| 1 cup, *cappelleti*, uncooked | = 90g |
| 1 cup, *casarecce*, boiled | = 136g |
| 1 cup, *casarecce*, uncooked | = 105g |
| 1 cup, *elbow*, boiled | = 140g |
| 1 cup, *elbow*, uncooked | = 105g |
| 1 cup, *fettucine*, boiled | = 140g |
| 1 cup, *fusilli*, boiled | = 120g |
| 1 cup, *fusilli*, uncooked | = 96g |
| 1 cup, *gnocchi*, boiled | = 127g |
| 1 cup, *gnocchi*, uncooked | = 96g |
| 1 cup, *gramigna*, boiled | = 154g |
| 1 cup, *gramigna*, uncooked | = 110g |
| 1 cup, *penne rigate*, boiled | = 113g |
| 1 cup, *penne rigate*, uncooked | = 102g |
| 1 cup, *rigatoni*, boiled | = 88g |
| 1 cup, *rigatoni*, uncooked | = 82g |
| 1 cup, *route*, boiled | = 101g |
| 1 cup, *route*, uncooked | = 78g |

# CEREALS, ROOTS, TUBERS and PRODUCTS

Figure 4. *Uncooked fusilli pasta*

Figure 5. *Uncooked gramigna pasta*

Figure 6. *Uncooked shell tri-color pasta*

# CEREALS, ROOTS, TUBERS and PRODUCTS

## PASTA

| | |
|---|---|
| 1 cup, *salad*, boiled | = 107g |
| 1 cup, *salad*, uncooked | = 100g |
| 1 cup, *shell* tricolor, large variety, boiled | = 128g |
| 1 cup, *shell* tricolor, large variety, uncooked | = 78g |
| 1 cup, *shell*, small variety, boiled | = 140g |
| 1 cup, *shell*, small variety, uncooked | = 105g |
| | |
| 1 cup, *sigarette ziti*, boiled | = 90g |
| 1 cup, *sigarette ziti*, uncooked | = 87g |
| 1 cup, *spaghetti*, boiled | = 140g |
| 1 cup, *spaghetti* spinach, boiled | = 150g |
| 1 cup, *spiral*, boiled | = 116g |
| 1 cup, *spiral*, uncooked | = 78g |
| | |
| 1 cup, *tortellini*, boiled | = 115g |
| 1 cup, *tortellini*, uncooked | = 96g |
| 1 cup, *tortiglioni*, boiled | = 85g |
| 1 cup, *tortiglioni*, uncooked | = 80g |

## POTATO

| | |
|---|---|
| 1 small pc. 1 ¾ to 2 ½ inch diam, yellow, with skin, raw | = 170g |
| 1 md pc. 2 ¼ to 3 ¼ inch diam, yellow, with skin, raw | = 213g |
| 1 large pc 3 ½ to 4 inch diam, yellow, with skin, raw | = 369g |
| | |
| 1 small pc. 1 ¾ to 2 ½ inch diam, yellow, with skin, baked | = 138g |
| 1 md pc. 2 ¼ to 3 ¼ inch diam, yellow, with skin, baked | = 172g |
| 1 large pc 3 ½ to 4 inch diam, yellow, with skin, baked | = 299g |
| | |
| 1 sm. pc. 1 ¾ to 2 ½ inch diam, yellow, without skin, boiled | = 125g |
| 1 md pc. 2 ¼ to 3 ¼ inch diam, yellow, without skin, boiled | = 167g |
| 1 large pc 3 ½ to 4 inch diam, yellow, without skin, boiled | = 300g |

# CEREALS, ROOTS, TUBERS and PRODUCTS

## POTATO

| | |
|---|---:|
| 1 piece, French cut, peeled, raw | = 8g |
| 1 cup, yellow, peeled, julienne cut, raw | = 160g |
| 1 cup, yellow, peeled, small dice ½ inch, raw | = 157g |
| 1 cup, yellow, peeled, medium dice ¾ inch, raw | = 145g |
| 1 cup, yellow, peeled, large dice 1-inch, raw | = 150g |
| 1 cup, yellow, hash brown, uncooked | = 159g |
| 1 cup, boiled, peeled, mashed, firmly packed | = 156g |
| 1 chip, dried potato, deep-fried | = 2g |
| | |
| 1 cup, flour, stirred, firmly packed | = 167g |
| 1 cup, flour, stirred, loosely packed | = 149g |
| 1 cup, instant soup, dry mix | = 117g |

## QUINOA

| | |
|---|---:|
| 1 cup, cooked | = 185g |
| 1 cup, uncooked | = 170g |
| 1 cup, flour, stirred, spooned | = 122g |
| 1 cup, flour, unstirred, spooned | = 131g |

## RICE

| | |
|---|---:|
| 1 cup, *brown, long-grain*, boiled | = 195g |
| 1 cup, *brown, long-grain*, uncooked | = 200g |
| 1 cup, *brown, medium-grain*, boiled | = 190g |
| 1 cup, *brown, medium-grain*, uncooked | = 195g |
| 1 cup, *brown, short-grain*, boiled | = 185g |
| 1 cup, *brown, short-grain*, uncooked | = 200g |
| | |
| 1 cup, *white, long-grain*, boiled | = 160g |
| 1 cup, *white, long-grain*, uncooked | = 185g |
| 1 cup, *white, long-grain*, parboiled, cooked | = 160g |
| 1 cup, *white, long-grain*, parboiled, dry | = 185g |

# CEREALS, ROOTS, TUBERS and PRODUCTS

### RICE

| | |
|---|---|
| 1 cup, *white, medium-grain*, boiled | = 195g |
| 1cup, *white, medium-grain*, uncooked | = 185g |
| 1 cup, *white, short-grain*, boiled | = 190g |
| 1 cup, *white, short-grain*, uncooked | = 200g |
| | |
| 1 cup, *flour*, stirred | = 108g |
| 1 cup, *flour*, unstirred | = 122g |
| 1 cup, *crispies*, rolled | = 100g |
| 1 cup, *crispies*, whole | = 40g |
| 1 cup, *bran*, toasted | = 118g |
| | |
| 1 cup, *white, glutinous*, cooked | = 175g |
| 1 cup, *white, glutinous*, cooked w/ coconut milk, sweetened | = 262g |
| 1 cup, *white, glutinous*, uncooked | = 185g |
| 1 cup, *white, glutinous*, coarsely ground, uncooked | = 184g |
| 1 cup, *white, glutinous*, flour, stirred | = 100g |
| 1 cup, *white, glutinous*, flour, unstirred | = 117g |

### SWEET POTATO

| | |
|---|---|
| 1 extra-small piece tuber, with skin, raw | = 67g |
| 1 small piece tuber, with skin, raw | = 100g |
| 1 medium piece tuber, with skin, raw | = 200g |
| 1 large piece tuber, with skin, raw | = 500g |
| | |
| 1 cup coarsely chopped, peeled, raw | = 155g |
| 1 cup cut into strips, 2 ½ to 3 inches long, peeled, raw | = 155g |
| 1 cup cut into rounds with ¾ inch thick, peeled, raw | = 150g |
| 1 cup, sliced ¼ inch thick, peeled, raw | = 155g |
| 1cup, minced, peeled, raw | = 145g |

# CEREALS, ROOTS, TUBERS and PRODUCTS

## SWEET POTATO
| | |
|---|---|
| 1 piece small tuber, with skin, boiled | = 98g |
| 1 piece medium tuber, with skin, boiled | = 194g |
| 1 piece large tuber, with skin, boiled | = 490g |
| | |
| 1 cup coarsely chopped, peeled, boiled | = 152g |
| 1 cup cut into strips, 2 ½ to 3 inches long, peeled, boiled | = 148g |
| 1 cup cut into rounds with ¾ inch thick, peeled, boiled | = 143g |
| 1 cup, sliced ¼ inch thick, peeled, boiled | = 174g |
| 1 cup, minced, peeled, boiled | = 139g |
| | |
| 1 cup coarsely chopped, peeled, fried | = 147g |
| 1 cup cut into strips, 2 ½ to 3 inches long, peeled, fried | = 150g |
| 1 cup cut into rounds with ¾ inch thick, peeled, fried | = 142g |
| 1 cup, sliced ¼ inch thick, peeled, fried | = 163g |
| 1 cup, minced, peeled, fried | = 158g |

## SUNCHOKE (JERUSALEM ARTICHOKE)
| | |
|---|---|
| 1 cup, peeled, sliced, raw | = 150g |

## TAPIOCA
| | |
|---|---|
| 1 cup, pearl, dried, large size, raw | = 300g |
| 1 cup, pearl, boiled, large size | = 201g |
| 1 cup, pearl, dried, small size, raw | = 307g |
| 1 cup, pearl, boiled, small size | = 216g |

## TARO
| | |
|---|---|
| 1 small tuber, whole, with skin, raw | = 67g |
| 1 medium tuber, whole, with skin, raw | = 100g |
| 1 large tuber, whole, with skin, raw | = 200g |
| 1 extra-large tuber, whole, with skin, raw | = 1000g |

# CEREALS, ROOTS, TUBERS and PRODUCTS

### TARO

| | |
|---|---|
| 1 cup, peeled, diced into 1-inch, raw | = 137g |
| 1 cup, peeled, diced into 1-inch, boiled | = 130g |
| 1 cup, peeled, sliced into ¼ inch thick, raw | = 149g |
| 1 cup, peeled, sliced into ¼ inch thick, boiled | = 145g |
| 1 cup, peeled, boiled, mashed | = 236g |

### TARO, SWAMP VARIETY (GALIANG)

| | |
|---|---|
| 1 extra-small tuber, whole, with skin, raw | = 250g |
| 1 small tuber, whole, with skin, raw | = 335g |
| 1 medium tuber, whole, with skin, raw | = 500g |
| 1 large tuber, whole with skin, raw | = 1000g |
| 1 cup, peeled, diced into 1-inch, raw | = 136g |
| 1 cup, peeled, diced into 1-inch, boiled | = 130g |
| 1 cup, peeled, sliced into ¼ inch thick, raw | = 142g |
| 1 cup, peeled, sliced into ¼ inch thick, boiled | = 147g |
| 1 cup, peeled, boiled, mashed | = 234g |

### WHEAT

| | |
|---|---|
| 1 cup, *bran*, raw | = 58g |
| 1 cup, *germ*, raw | = 115g |
| 1 cup, *germ*, toasted | = 110g |
| 1 cup, *sprouted*, uncooked | = 108g |
| 1 cup, *flour, all purpose*, sifted, dipped | = 129g |
| 1 cup, *flour, all purpose*, sifted, spooned | = 120g |
| 1 cup, *flour, all purpose*, unsifted, dipped | = 146g |
| 1 cup, *flour, all purpose*, unsifted, spooned | = 127g |

# CEREALS, ROOTS, TUBERS and PRODUCTS

## WHEAT

| | |
|---|---|
| 1 cup, *flour, bread*, sifted, dipped | = 130g |
| 1 cup, *flour, bread*, sifted, spooned | = 105g |
| 1 cup, *flour, bread*, unsifted, dipped | = 150g |
| 1 cup, *flour, bread*, sifted, spooned | = 126g |
| | |
| 1 cup, *flour, cake*, sifted, dipped | = 135g |
| 1 cup, *flour, cake*, sifted, spooned | = 125g |
| 1 cup, *flour, cake*, unsifted, dipped | = 144g |
| 1 cup, *flour, cake*, unsifted, spooned | = 135g |
| 1 cup, *flour, whole wheat*, stirred, spooned | = 150g |
| 1 cup, *flour, whole wheat*, unstirred, dipped | = 170g |
| 1 cup, *flour, whole wheat*, unstirred, spooned | = 160g |

## YAM

| | |
|---|---|
| 1 cup, purple, peeled, diced into 1-inch, raw | = 150g |
| 1 cup, purple, peeled, diced into 1-inch, boiled | = 136g |
| 1 small tuber, spiny, whole, with skin, raw | = 100g |
| 1 medium tuber, spiny, whole, with skin, raw | = 150g |
| 1 large tuber, spiny, whole, with skin, raw | = 200g |

## YAUTIA

| | |
|---|---|
| 1 extra-small tuber, whole, with skin, raw | =  65g |
| 1 small tuber, whole, with skin, raw | = 100g |
| 1 medium tuber, whole, with skin, raw | = 200 |
| 1 large tuber, whole with skin, raw | = 350g |
| | |
| 1 cup, peeled, diced into 1-inch, raw | = 142g |
| 1 cup, peeled, diced into 1-inch, boiled | = 138g |
| 1 cup, peeled, sliced into ¼ inch thick, raw | = 145g |
| 1 cup, peeled, sliced into ¼ inch thick, boiled | = 140g |
| 1 cup, peeled, boiled, mashed | = 240g |

# FRUITS and FRUIT PRODUCTS

# FRUITS and FRUIT PRODUCTS

### ACEROLA (WEST INDIAN CHERRY)

| | |
|---|---|
| 1 cup, whole fruit, raw | =  98g |
| 1 cup, juice, raw | = 242g |

### APPLE (COMPOSITE)

| | |
|---|---|
| 1 extra small, 2 ½ inches diam, raw, with skin | = 101g |
| 1 extra small, 2 ½ inches diam, raw, peeled | =  88g |
| 1 small, 2 ¾ inches diam, raw, with skin | = 149g |
| 1 small, 2 ¾ inches diam, raw, peeled | = 132g |
| | |
| 1 medium, 3 inches diam, raw, with skin | = 182g |
| 1 medium, 3 inches diam, raw, peeled | = 161g |
| 1 large, 3 ¼ inches diam, raw, with skin | = 223g |
| 1 large, 3 ¼ inches diam, raw, peeled | = 216g |
| | |
| 1 cup, peeled, medium dice ¾ inch, raw | = 155g |
| 1 cup, peeled, medium dice ¾ inch, boiled | = 180g |
| 1 cup, peeled, thinly sliced, raw | = 110g |
| 1 cup, peeled, thinly sliced, boiled | = 170g |
| | |
| 1 cup, *fresh juice*, unsweetened, undiluted | = 250g |
| 1 cup, *fruit*, canned, sweetened, sliced, drained | = 204g |
| 1 cup, *dried fruit*, sulfured, stewed with sugar | = 280g |
| 1 cup, *dried fruit*, sulfured, stewed, without sugar | = 255g |
| 1 cup, *sauce*, canned, sweetened | = 255g |
| 1 cup *sauce*, canned, unsweetened | = 240g |

### APPLE, FUJI

| | |
|---|---|
| 1 small, raw, whole, with skin | = 158g |
| 1 medium, raw, whole, with skin | = 192g |
| 1 large, raw, whole, with skin | = 236g |

# FRUITS and FRUIT PRODUCTS

## APPLE, GALA
|   |   |
|---|---|
| 1 small, raw, whole, with skin | = 157g |
| 1 medium, raw, whole, with skin | = 172g |
| 1 large, raw, whole, with skin | = 200g |

## APPLE, GRANNY SMITH
|   |   |
|---|---|
| 1 small, raw, whole, with skin | = 144g |
| 1 medium, raw, whole, with skin | = 167g |
| 1 large, raw, whole, with skin | = 206g |

## APPLE, GOLDEN DELICIOUS
|   |   |
|---|---|
| 1 small, raw, whole, with skin | = 129g |
| 1 medium, raw, whole, with skin | = 169g |
| 1 large, raw, whole, with skin | = 215g |

## APPLE, RED DELICIOUS
|   |   |
|---|---|
| 1 small, raw, whole, with skin | = 158g |
| 1 medium, raw, whole, with skin | = 212g |
| 1 large, raw, whole, with skin | = 260g |

## APRICOT
|   |   |
|---|---|
| 1 medium, raw, whole with skin | = 32g |
| 1 large, raw, whole, with skin | = 38g |
| 1 jumbo, raw, whole, with skin | = 45g |
| 1 extra jumbo, raw, whole, with skin | = 56g |
| 1 cup, raw, peeled, thinly sliced | = 224g |
| 1 cup, raw, peeled, halves | = 155g |
| 1 piece, halves, canned, with skin, in water pack | = 36g |
| 1 piece, halves, canned, with skin, in juice pack | = 36g |
| 1 piece, halves, canned, with skin, in light syrup | = 40g |
| 1 piece, halves, canned, with skin, in heavy syrup | = 40g |

# FRUITS and FRUIT PRODUCTS

**APRICOT**

| | |
|---|---|
| 1 cup, dehydrated, sulfured, uncooked | = 119g |
| 1 cup, dehydrated, sulfured, stewed | = 249g |
| 1 cup, nectar, canned | = 250g |

**AVOCADO**

| | |
|---|---|
| 1 small fruit, raw, whole, with skin and stone | = 165g |
| 1 small fruit, raw, no skin and stone | = 112g |
| 1 medium fruit, raw, whole, with skin and stone | = 250g |
| 1 medium fruit, raw, no skin and stone | = 170g |
| 1 large fruit, raw, whole, with skin and stone | = 300g |
| 1 large fruit, raw, no skin and stone | = 200g |
| 1 extra-large, raw, whole, with skin and stone | = 500g |
| 1 extra-large, raw, no skin and stone | = 340g |
| | |
| 1 cup, raw, pulp, thinly sliced | = 150g |
| 1 cup, raw, pulp, medium diced ¾ inch | = 150g |
| 1 cup, raw, pulp, pureed | = 240g |

**BANANA, BONGOLAN**

| | |
|---|---|
| 1 small fruit, whole, raw, with skin | = 50g |
| 1 medium fruit, whole, raw, with skin | = 63g |
| 1 large fruit, whole, raw, with skin | = 83g |
| 1 extra-large fruit, whole, raw, with skin | = 125g |

**BANANA, CAVENDISH**

| | |
|---|---|
| 1 small fruit, whole, raw, with skin | = 83g |
| 1 medium fruit, whole, raw, with skin | = 100g |
| 1 large fruit, whole, raw, with skin | = 125g |
| 1 extra-large fruit, whole, raw, with skin | = 167g |
| 1 cup, ripe, peeled, thinly sliced, raw | = 150g |
| 1 cup, ripe, peeled, mashed, raw | = 225g |

# FRUITS and FRUIT PRODUCTS

### BANANA, LACATAN

| | |
|---|---|
| 1 small fruit, whole, raw, with skin | = 55g |
| 1 medium fruit, whole, raw, with skin | = 67g |
| 1 large fruit, whole, raw, with skin | = 83g |
| 1 extra-large fruit, whole, raw, with skin | = 125g |
| 1 cup, ripe, peeled, thinly sliced, raw | = 150g |
| 1 cup, ripe, peeled, medium diced, raw | = 165g |
| 1 cup, ripe, peeled, mashed, raw | = 238g |

### BANANA, LATUNDAN

| | |
|---|---|
| 1 small fruit, whole, raw, with skin | = 50g |
| 1 medium fruit, whole, raw, with skin | = 60g |
| 1 large fruit, whole, raw, with skin | = 80g |
| 1 extra-large fruit, whole, raw, with skin | = 100g |
| 1 cup, ripe, peeled, thinly sliced, raw | = 153g |
| 1 cup, ripe, peeled, medium diced, raw | = 168g |
| 1 cup, ripe, peeled, mashed, raw | = 238g |

### BANANA, SABA

| | |
|---|---|
| 1 small fruit, whole, raw, with skin | = 50g |
| 1 medium fruit, whole, raw, with skin | = 63g |
| 1 large fruit, whole, raw, with skin | = 83g |
| 1 extra-large fruit, whole, raw, with skin | = 125g |
| 1 cup, ripe, peeled, cut diagonally 1" long | = 129g |
| 1 cup, unripe, chips, deep-fried, sweetened | = 85g |

# FRUITS and FRUIT PRODUCTS

**BILIMBI**

| | |
|---|---|
| 1 small fruit, whole, raw | = 14g |
| 1 medium fruit, whole, raw | = 22g |
| 1 large, whole, raw | = 33g |
| 1 cup, whole fruit, raw | = 152g |
| 1 cup, whole fruit, boiled | = 178g |
| 1 cup, boiled, mashed | = 231g |

**BLACKBERRY**

| | |
|---|---|
| 1 cup, whole, raw | = 140g |
| 1 cup, whole, canned, in light syrup | = 240g |
| 1 cup, whole, canned, in heavy syrup | = 250g |
| 1 cup, juice, canned, diluted, sweetened | = 250g |

**BLUEBERRY**

| | |
|---|---|
| 1 small fruit, whole, raw | = 4g |
| 1 medium fruit, whole, raw | = 6g |
| 1 large fruit, whole, raw | = 8g |
| 1 extra-large fruit, whole, raw | = 10g |
| | |
| 1 cup, whole, raw | = 155g |
| 1 cup, whole, dried, sweetened | = 160g |
| 1 cup, whole, canned in light syrup | = 244g |
| 1 cup, whole, canned in heavy syrup | = 256g |

**BOYSENBERRY**

| | |
|---|---|
| 1 cup, canned in heavy syrup, drained | = 256g |

**BREADFRUIT**

| | |
|---|---|
| 1 cup, peeled, sliced, raw | = 220g |

# FRUITS and FRUIT PRODUCTS

## BREADNUT

| | |
|---|---|
| 1 extra-small fruit, whole, raw | = 670g |
| 1 small fruit, whole, raw | = 1300g |
| 1 medium fruit, whole, raw | = 1500g |
| 1 large fruit, whole, raw | = 3000g |
| 1 extra-large fruit, whole, raw | = 6000g |
| | |
| 1 cup, immature fruit, peeled, thinly sliced, raw | = 104g |
| 1 cup, immature fruit, peeled, thinly sliced, boiled | = 122g |
| 1 cup, immature fruit, peeled, diced, raw | = 132g |
| 1 cup, immature fruit, peeled, diced, boiled | = 158g |
| 1 cup, ripe fruit, peeled and seeded, thinly sliced, raw | = 206g |

## CALAMANSI (PHILIPPINE LEMON)

| | |
|---|---|
| 1 small fruit, whole, with skin and seeds | = 10g |
| 1 medium fruit, whole, with skin and seeds | = 15g |
| 1 large fruit, whole, with skin and seeds | = 20g |
| 1 extra-large fruit, whole, with skin and seeds | = 25g |
| 1 cup, juice, undiluted, raw | = 237g |

## CANISTEL (TIESA)

| | |
|---|---|
| 1 small fruit, whole, with skin | = 125g |
| 1 medium fruit, whole, with skin | = 143g |
| 1 large fruit, whole, with skin | = 167g |
| 1 cup, peeled and seeded, cubed, raw | = 150g |
| 1 cup, peeled and seeded, mashed, raw | = 228g |

## CARAMBOLA (STAR FRUIT)

| | |
|---|---|
| 1 extra small fruit, whole, with skin and seeds | = 33g |
| 1 small fruit, whole, with skin and seeds | = 70g |
| 1 medium fruit, whole, with skin and seeds | = 90g |

# FRUITS and FRUIT PRODUCTS

### CARAMBOLA (STAR FRUIT)

| | |
|---|---|
| 1 large fruit, whole, with skin and seeds | = 124g |
| 1 extra-large fruit, whole, with skin and seeds | = 200g |
| 1 cup, medium diced ¾ inches, raw | = 135g |
| 1 cup, sliced, raw | = 115g |

### CARISSA (KARANDA)

| | |
|---|---|
| 1 cup, skinned and seeded, halves, raw | = 150g |

### CHERIMOYA

| | |
|---|---|
| 1 cup, skinned and seeded, sliced, raw | = 160g |

### CHERRY

| | |
|---|---|
| 1 piece | =   8g |
| 1 cup, sour, red, raw with pits | = 103g |
| 1 cup, sour, red, raw without pits | = 155g |
| 1 cup, sweet, red, raw with pits | = 138g |
| 1 cup, sweet, red, raw, without pits | = 154g |
| 1 cup, bottled, in water, without pits | = 250g |
| 1 cup, bottled, in light syrup, without pits | = 250g |
| 1 cup, bottled, in heavy syrup, without pits | = 260g |

### CRANBERRY

| | |
|---|---|
| 1 cup, whole, with skin, raw | = 100g |
| 1 cup, whole, with skin, chopped | = 110g |
| 1 cup, dried, sweetened | = 120g |
| 1 cup, sauce, canned, sweetened | = 277g |
| 1 cup, juice, canned, unsweetened | = 253g |

# FRUITS and FRUIT PRODUCTS

**Figure 7.** *Peeled, seeded and chopped canistel fruit*

# FRUITS and FRUIT PRODUCTS

## COCONUT

| | |
|---|---|
| 1 cup, immature flesh, shredded, raw | = 204g |
| 1 cup, coconut water, fresh | = 246g |
| 1 cup, mature coconut meat, grated, raw, loosely packed | = 80g |
| 1 cup, coconut cream, raw (liquid from grated meat) | = 256g |
| 1 cup, coconut milk, freshly squeezed with added water | = 232g |
| 1 cup, coconut milk, canned | = 226g |

## COCONUT SPORT (MACAPUNO)

| | |
|---|---|
| 1 cup, bottled, sweetened | = 228g |

## CUSTARD APLE

| | |
|---|---|
| 1 small fruit, whole, with skin and seeds | = 85g |
| 1 medium fruit, whole, with skin and seeds | = 140g |
| 1 large fruit, whole, with skin and seeds | = 200g |
| 1 extra-large fruit, whole, with skin and seeds | = 400g |
| 1 cup, pulp, no skin and seeded, raw, firmly packed | = 270g |
| 1 cup, pulp, no skin and seeded, raw, loosely packed | = 235g |

## CURRANTS

| | |
|---|---|
| 1 cup, black, raw | = 112g |
| 1 cup, red, raw | = 118g |
| 1 cup, zante, dried | = 144g |
| 1 cup, red, jellied, bottled | = 320g |

## DATES

| | |
|---|---|
| 1 piece, dried, with pits | = 24g |
| 1 cup, dried, pitted, sweetened, chopped, firmly packed | = 180g |
| 1 cup, dried, pitted, sweetened, whole, firmly packed | = 240g |
| 1 cup, dried, pitted, sweetened, whole, loosely packed | = 155g |

# FRUITS and FRUIT PRODUCTS

**Figure 8.** *Loosely packed, dried, pitted dates*

**Figure 9.** *Firmly packed, dried, pitted dates*

# FRUITS and FRUIT PRODUCTS

## DURIAN

| | |
|---|---|
| 1 small fruit, whole, with skin and seeds | = 1000g |
| 1 medium fruit, whole, with skin and seeds | = 2000g |
| 1 large fruit, whole, with skin and seeds | = 5000g |
| 1 cup, raw, peeled and seeded, medium diced | = 260g |
| 1 cup, raw, peeled and seeded, large diced 1-inch | = 240g |

## FEIJOA (PINEAPPLE GUAVA)

| | |
|---|---|
| 1 medium fruit, whole with skin, raw | = 55g |
| 1 cup, peeled, chopped into 1-inch | = 218g |
| 1 cup, peeled, thinly sliced | = 226g |
| 1 cup, pureed, unsweetened, raw | = 254g |
| 1 cup, pureed, sweetened, stewed | = 332g |

## FIGS

| | |
|---|---|
| 1 small, 1 ½ inch diameter, raw | = 40g |
| 1 medium, 2 ¼ inch diameter, raw | = 50g |
| 1 large, 2 ½ inch diameter, raw | = 64g |
| 1 cup, dried, uncooked | = 150g |
| 1 cup, dried, stewed | = 260g |
| 1 piece, dried | = 8g |
| 1 piece, canned, in water pack | = 27g |
| 1 piece, canned, in light syrup | = 28g |
| 1 cup, canned, in water pack | = 248g |
| 1 cup, canned, in light syrup | = 252g |
| 1 cup, canned in heavy syrup | = 259g |
| 1 cup, canned in extra heavy syrup | = 261g |

# FRUITS and FRUIT PRODUCTS

## FRUIT COCKTAIL

| | |
|---|---|
| 1 cup, canned in juice pack | = 237g |
| 1 cup, canned, in light syrup | = 242g |
| 1 cup, canned, in heavy syrup | = 248g |
| 1 cup, canned in extra heavy syrup | = 260g |

## GOOSEBERRIES

| | |
|---|---|
| 1 cup, whole, raw | = 235g |
| 1 cup, canned in light syrup, drained | = 255g |

## GRAPES

| | |
|---|---|
| 1 piece, whole, raw, seeded | = 5g |
| 1 piece, whole, raw, seedless | = 4g |
| 1 cup, whole, raw, seeded | = 170g |
| 1 cup, whole, raw seedless | = 165g |
| 1 cup, whole, canned, seedless in water pack | = 245g |
| 1 cup, whole, canned, seedless in heavy syrup | = 260g |
| 1 cup, juice, canned, unsweetened, undiluted | = 250g |

## GRAPEFRUIT

| | |
|---|---|
| 1 fruit, 3 ¾ inches diameter, whole, raw | = 246g |
| 1 cup, juice, raw | = 250g |
| 1 cup, sectioned, raw | = 230g |
| 1 cup, sectioned, canned, in water pack | = 245g |
| 1 cup, sectioned, canned, in juice pack | = 250g |
| 1 cup, sectioned, canned, in light pack | = 255g |

## GUAVA APPLE

| | |
|---|---|
| 1 small fruit, whole, with skin, raw | = 250g |
| 1 medium fruit, whole, with skin, raw | = 333g |
| 1 large fruit, whole, with skin, raw | = 500g |

# FRUITS and FRUIT PRODUCTS

## GUAVA

| | | |
|---|---|---|
| 1 small fruit, whole, with skin, raw | = | 30g |
| 1 medium fruit, whole, with skin, raw | = | 50g |
| 1 large fruit, whole, with skin, raw | = | 65g |
| 1 extra-large, whole, with skin, raw | = | 100g |
| | | |
| 1 cup, pink flesh, ripe, with skin, raw, thinly sliced | = | 165g |
| 1 cup, pink flesh, ripe, peeled, raw, thinly sliced | = | 160g |
| 1 cup, white flesh, ripe, with skin, raw, thinly sliced | = | 155g |
| 1 cup, white flesh, ripe, peeled, raw, thinly sliced | = | 145g |
| | | |
| 1 cup, sauce, stewed | = | 240g |
| 1 cup, nectar, canned | = | 250g |
| 1 cup, pureed, sweetened, bottled | = | 320g |

## JACKFRUIT

| | | |
|---|---|---|
| 1 cup, ripe, whole, seeded | = | 197g |
| 1 cup, ripe, cut into strips | = | 212g |
| 1 cup, ripe, seeded, medium diced | = | 175g |
| 1 cup, canned, seeded, whole, in heavy syrup | = | 237g |

## JAVA PLUM

| | | |
|---|---|---|
| 1 small fruit, whole, with skin and stone | = | 7g |
| 1 medium fruit, whole, with skin and stone | = | 10g |
| 1 large fruit, whole, with skin and stone | = | 15g |
| 1 cup, whole, with skin and stone, raw | = | 147g |

## JUJUBE

| | | |
|---|---|---|
| 1 medium fruit, whole with skin, raw | = | 78g |

# FRUITS and FRUIT PRODUCTS

## KIWIFRUIT

| | |
|---|---|
| 1 piece, green, whole, with skin, raw | = 70g |
| 1 cup, green peeled, sliced, raw | = 180g |
| 1 cup, green, peeled, medium diced ¾ inch, raw | = 180g |
| 1 cup, green, peeled, large diced 1-inch, raw | = 170g |
| | |
| 1 piece, gold, whole, with skin, raw | = 86g |
| 1 cup, gold, peeled, sliced, raw | = 186g |
| 1 cup, gold, peeled, medium diced ¾ inch, raw | = 186g |
| 1 cup, gold, peeled, large diced 1-inch, raw | = 175g |

## KUM QUAT

| | |
|---|---|
| 1 small fruit, round, with skin and seeds | = 25g |
| 1 medium fruit, round, with skin and seeds | = 40g |
| 1 large fruit, round, with skin and seeds | = 60g |
| 1 cup, peeled, sectioned, raw | = 170g |

## LANZON (PHILIPPINE NATIVE)

| | |
|---|---|
| 1 small fruit, whole, with skin and seeds | = 12g |
| 1 medium fruit, whole, with skin and seeds | = 14g |
| 1 large fruit, whole, with skin and seeds | = 17g |
| 1 cup, fruit, peeled, segmented, raw | = 192g |

## LANZON (SULO VARIETY)

| | |
|---|---|
| 1 small fruit, whole, with skin and seeds | = 28g |
| 1 medium fruit, whole, with skin and seeds | = 30g |
| 1 large fruit, whole, with skin and seeds | = 33g |

## LANZON (DUCO VARIETY)

| | |
|---|---|
| 1 small fruit, whole, with skin and seeds | = 20g |
| 1 medium fruit, whole, with skin and seeds | = 23g |
| 1 large fruit, whole, with skin and seeds | = 25g |

# FRUITS and FRUIT PRODUCTS

**Figure 10.** *Seeded ripe jackfruit*

# FRUITS and FRUIT PRODUCTS

## LEMON

| | |
|---|---|
| 1 small fruit, whole, with skin and seeds | = 67g |
| 1 medium fruit, whole, with skin and seeds | = 80g |
| 1 large fruit, whole, with skin and seeds | = 100g |
| | |
| 1 cup, sectioned, raw, without peel | = 212g |
| 1 cup, peel, raw | = 96g |
| 1 cup, juice, raw | = 244g |

## LIME

| | |
|---|---|
| 1 small fruit, whole, with skin and seeds | = 40g |
| 1 medium fruit, whole, with skin and seeds | = 55g |
| 1 large fruit, whole, with skin and seeds | = 84g |
| | |
| 1 cup, juice, raw | = 242g |
| 1 cup, juice, bottled, sweetened | = 246g |
| 1 cup, juice, bottled, unsweetened | = 240g |

## LIPOTE

| | |
|---|---|
| 1 cup, whole, with skin and seeds, raw | = 152g |

## LOGANBERRIES

| | |
|---|---|
| 1 cup, whole, raw | = 147g |

## LONGAN

| | |
|---|---|
| 1 cup, peeled, with stone, loosely packed | = 207g |
| 1 cup, peeled, pitted, raw, firmly packed | = 236g |
| 1 cup, peeled, pitted, raw, loosely packed | = 194g |
| 1 cup, canned, pitted, in water pack, drained | = 163g |

## LOQUATS

| | |
|---|---|
| 1 cup, peeled and seeded, chopped, raw | = 149g |

# FRUITS and FRUIT PRODUCTS

**Figure 11.** *Peeled, with pits longan fruits*

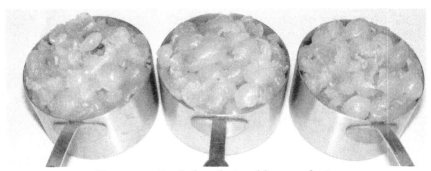

**Figure 12.** *Peeled and pitted longan fruits*

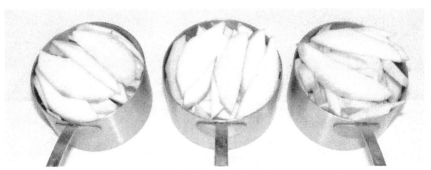

**Figure 13.** *Peeled and seeded, thinly sliced, unripe indian mango*

# FRUITS and FRUIT PRODUCTS

## LYCHEE (LITCHI)

| | |
|---|---|
| 1 piece, whole, raw, with pit | = 10g |
| 1 cup, whole, raw, with pit | = 190g |
| 1 piece, dried, pitted | = 6g |
| 1 cup, canned, pitted, drained, firmly packed | = 219g |
| 1 cup, canned, pitted, drained, loosely packed | =194g |

## MANGO, CARABAO

| | |
|---|---|
| 1 small ripe fruit, whole, with skin and seed | = 143g |
| 1 medium ripe fruit, whole, with skin and seed | = 200g |
| 1 large ripe fruit, whole, with skin and seed | = 500g |
| 1 cup, ripe, medium diced ¾ inch, raw | = 200g |
| 1 cup, ripe, puree, raw | = 242g |
| 1 cup, ripe, thinly sliced, raw | = 195g |
| 1 cup, unripe, peeled, minced, raw, firmly packed | = 175g |
| 1 cup, unripe, peeled, minced, raw, loosely packed | = 145g |
| 1 cup, unripe, peeled, sticks, raw | = 130g |
| 1 cup, unripe, peeled, thinly sliced, raw | = 125g |
| 1 cup, nectar, raw | = 250g |
| 1 cup, candied, diced | = 115g |
| 1 cup, dried, thinly sliced, firmly packed | = 235g |
| 1 cup, dried, thinly sliced, loosely packed | = 209g |
| 1 piece, dried, thinly sliced | = 15g |

## MANGO, HAWAIIAN

| | |
|---|---|
| 1 small fruit, whole with skin and seed | = 100g |
| 1 medium fruit, whole with skin and seed | = 135g |
| 1 large fruit, whole with skin and seed | = 200g |

# FRUITS and FRUIT PRODUCTS

### MANGO, INDIAN

| | |
|---|---|
| 1 small fruit, whole, with skin and seed | = 125g |
| 1 medium fruit, whole, with skin and seed | = 167g |
| 1 large fruit, whole, with skin and seed | = 250g |
| | |
| 1 cup, unripe, peeled, cut into sticks, raw | = 120g |
| 1 cup, unripe, peeled, thinly sliced, raw | = 115g |
| 1cup, unripe, peeled, minced, raw, firmly packed | = 150g |
| 1 cup, unripe, peeled, minced, raw, loosely packed | = 135g |

### MANGO, PICO

| | |
|---|---|
| 1 small fruit, whole, with skin and seed | = 125g |
| 1 medium fruit, whole, with skin and seed | = 167g |
| 1 large fruit, whole, with skin and seed | = 333g |

### MANGOSTEEN

| | |
|---|---|
| 1 small fruit, whole, with skin and seed | = 66g |
| 1 medium fruit, whole, with skin and seed | = 100g |
| 1 large fruit, whole, with skin and seed | = 200g |
| 1 cup, ripe pulp, skinned, segmented, raw | = 110g |
| 1 cup, canned, in light syrup, drained | = 210g |

### MARANG

| | |
|---|---|
| 1 small fruit, whole, with skin and seed | = 1000g |
| 1 medium fruit, whole, with skin and seed | = 1500g |
| 1 large fruit, whole, with skin and seed | = 2000g |

### MELON, CANTALOUPE

| | |
|---|---|
| 1 small, 4-inches diameter, whole, raw | = 500g |
| 1 medium, 5-inches diameter, whole, raw | = 750g |
| 1 large, 6-inches diameter, whole, raw | = 1000g |
| 1 extra-large, 7-inches diameter, whole, raw | = 1500g |

# FRUITS and FRUIT PRODUCTS

## MELON, CANTALOUPE
| | |
|---|---|
| 1 cup, cut into balls, raw | = 170g |
| 1 cup, medium diced ¾ inch, raw | = 160g |
| 1 cup, shredded, raw | = 212g |

## MELON, HONEYDEW
| | |
|---|---|
| 1 small, 4-inches diameter, whole, raw | = 750g |
| 1 medium, 5-inches diameter, whole, raw | = 1000g |
| 1 large, 6-inches diameter, whole, raw | = 1250g |
| 1 cup, cut into balls, raw | = 180g |
| 1 cup, medium diced ¾ inch, raw | = 170g |
| 1 cup, shredded, raw | = 224g |

## MELON, WATERMELON
| | |
|---|---|
| 1 cup, medium diced ¾ inch, raw | = 153g |
| 1 cup, cut into balls, raw | = 166g |

## MULBERRIES
| | |
|---|---|
| 1 cup, whole, raw | = 140g |

## NANCE (YELLOW CHERRIES)
| | |
|---|---|
| 1 cup, pitted, raw | = 112g |

## NECTARINES
| | |
|---|---|
| 1 small fruit, whole with skin and seed, raw | = 129g |
| 1 medium fruit, whole with skin and seed, raw | = 142g |
| 1 cup, peeled and seeded, thinly sliced, raw | = 143g |

## NATA DE COCO
| | |
|---|---|
| 1 cup, cubed, raw | = 172g |
| 1 cup, cubed, bottled, sweetened | = 196g |

# FRUITS and FRUIT PRODUCTS

## ORANGE, MANDARIN

| | |
|---|---|
| 1 piece fruit, *Batangas variety* | = 125g |
| 1 piece fruit, *King variety* | = 250g |
| | |
| 1 small fruit, *Lado variety*, whole, with skin and seeds | = 100g |
| 1 medium fruit, *Lado variety*, whole, with skin and seeds | = 111g |
| 1 large fruit fruit, *Lado variety*, whole, with skin and seeds | = 125g |
| | |
| 1 piece fruit, *Laon variety* | = 143g |
| 1 piece fruit, Tizon variety, whole, with skin and seeds | = 200g |
| | |
| 1 small fruit, *Szinkon variety*, whole with skin and seeds | = 77g |
| 1 medium fruit, *Szinkon variety*, whole with skin and seeds | = 100g |
| 1 large fruit, *Szinkon variety*, whole with skin and seeds | = 167g |
| | |
| 1 small fruit, *Taikat variety*, whole with skin and seeds | = 67g |
| 1 medium fruit, *Taikat variety*, whole with skin and seeds | = 80g |
| 1 large fruit, *Taikat variety*, whole, with skin and seeds | = 100g |
| | |
| 1 small, whole, peeled, raw, with pips and membrane | = 76g |
| 1 medium, whole, peeled, raw, with pips and membrane | = 88g |
| 1 large, whole, peeled, raw, with pips and membrane | = 120g |
| | |
| 1 cup, sectioned, with pips and membrane, raw | = 200g |
| 1 cup, sectioned, no pips and membrane, raw | = 183g |
| 1 cup, sectioned, canned in light syrup | = 177g |
| | |
| 1 cup, juice, undiluted, unsweetened, raw | = 250g |
| 1 cup, juice, canned, sweetened | = 250g |

# FRUITS and FRUIT PRODUCTS

## ORANGE, PHILIPPINE NATIVE CAJEL

| | |
|---|---|
| 1 small fruit, whole with skin, raw | = 145g |
| 1 medium fruit, whole with skin, raw | = 200g |
| 1 large fruit, whole with skin, raw | = 250g |

## ORANGE, VALENCIA

| | |
|---|---|
| 1 small, whole with skin, 2 ½ inches diameter, raw | = 128g |
| 1 medium, whole with skin, 2 5/8 inches diameter, raw | = 175g |
| 1 large, whole with skin, 3-inches diameter, raw | = 245g |
| 1 extra-large whole, with skin, 3 ½ inches diameter, raw | = 300g |
| | |
| 1 small, whole, peeled, raw, with pips and membrane | = 102g |
| 1 medium, whole, peeled, raw, with pips and membrane | = 136g |
| 1 large, whole, peeled, raw, with pips and membrane | = 188g |
| 1 extra-large, whole, peeled, raw, with pips and membrane | = 220g |
| | |
| 1 cup, sectioned, with pips and membrane, raw | = 200g |
| 1 cup, sectioned, no pips and membrane, raw | = 175g |
| 1 cup, peel, raw, firmly packed | = 100g |
| 1 cup, peel, raw, minced, firmly packed | = 170g |
| | |
| 1 cup, juice, undiluted, unsweetened, raw | = 246g |
| 1 cup, juice, sweetened, raw | = 250g |
| 1 cup, juice, canned, unsweetened | = 250g |
| 1 cup, juice, canned, sweetened | = 250g |

# FRUITS and FRUIT PRODUCTS

## PAPAYA

| | |
|---|---|
| 1 extra-small, ripe, whole with skin and seeds, raw | = 245g |
| 1 small, ripe, whole, with skin and seeds, raw | = 470g |
| 1 medium, ripe, whole, with skin and seeds, raw | = 660g |
| 1 large, ripe, whole, with skin and seeds, raw | = 1220g |
| | |
| 1 cup, ripe, peeled and seeded, raw, cut into balls | = 175g |
| 1 cup, ripe, peeled and seeded, raw, diced 1-inch | = 146g |
| 1 cup, ripe, peeled and seeded, raw, diced ¾-inch | = 160g |
| 1 cup, ripe, peeled and seeded, raw, mashed | = 234g |
| 1 cup, nectar, canned | = 250g |

## PASSION FRUIT

| | |
|---|---|
| 1 cup, purple, raw | = 242g |

## PEACH

| | |
|---|---|
| 1 small, whole, with skin and seed, 2 ½ inches diam | = 130g |
| 1 medium, whole, with skin and seed, 2 2/3 inches diam | = 150g |
| 1 large, whole, with skin and seed, 2 ¾ inches diam | = 175g |
| 1 extra-large, whole, with skin and seed, 3 inches diam | = 224g |
| | |
| 1 cup, peeled and seeded, raw, medium diced ¾ inches | = 155g |
| 1 cup, peeled and seeded, raw, thinly sliced | = 162g |
| 1 cup, peeled and seeded, dried, uncooked | = 160g |
| 1 cup, peeled and seeded, dried, stewed, unsweetened | = 258g |
| 1 cup, peeled and seeded, dried, stewed, sweetened | = 270g |
| | |
| 1 cup, nectar, canned | = 250g |
| 1 cup, canned in water pack, sliced | = 244g |
| 1 cup, canned in juice pack, sliced | = 248g |
| 1 cup, canned in light syrup, sliced | = 251g |
| 1 cup, canned in heavy syrup, sliced | = 262g |

# FRUITS and FRUIT PRODUCTS

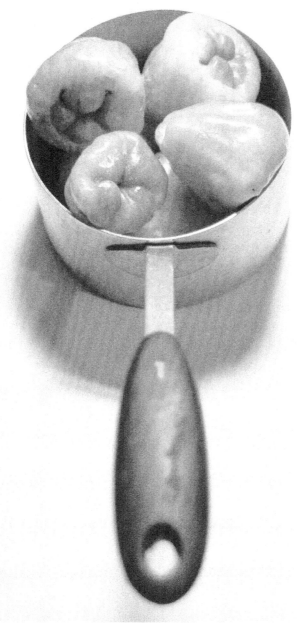

Figure 14. *Small rose apple fruits*

# FRUITS and FRUIT PRODUCTS

## PEAR

| | |
|---|---|
| 1 small fruit, whole, with skin, raw | = 135g |
| 1 medium fruit, whole, with skin, raw | = 167g |
| 1 large fruit, whole, with skin, raw | = 228g |
| | |
| 1 cup, peeled, raw diced 1-inch | = 160g |
| 1 cup, peeled, raw thinly sliced | = 155g |
| 1 cup, cooked, mashed | = 256g |
| 1 cup, canned, nectar | = 250g |
| | |
| 1 cup, dried, halves, uncooked | = 180g |
| 1 cup, dried, halves, cooked, unsweetened | = 255g |
| 1 cup, dried, halves, cooked, sweetened | = 280g |
| | |
| 1 cup, canned in water pack, cut in halves | = 244g |
| 1 cup, canned in water pack, diced | = 230g |
| 1 cup, canned in juice pack, cut in halves | = 248g |
| 1 cup, canned in juice pack, diced | = 232g |
| 1 cup, canned in light syrup, cut in halves | = 250g |
| | |
| 1 cup, canned in light syrup, diced | = 227g |
| 1 cup, canned in heavy syrup, cut in halves | = 280g |
| 1 cup, canned in heavy syrup, diced | = 265g |

## PERSIMMON

| | |
|---|---|
| 1 small fruit, whole, with skin, raw | = 196g |
| 1 medium fruit, whole, with skin, raw | = 255g |
| 1 cup, skinned, wedged, raw | = 169g |
| 1 cup, skinned, thinly sliced, raw | = 187g |

# FRUITS and FRUIT PRODUCTS

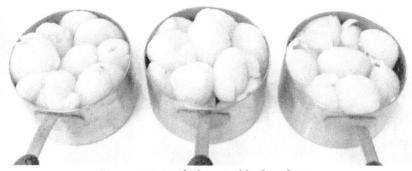

Figure 15. *Peeled, pitted lychee fruit*

Figure 16. *Thinly sliced, sweetened pears*

Figure 17. *Peeled, seeded star apple fruit*

# FRUITS and FRUIT PRODUCTS

## PINEAPPLE

| | |
|---|---|
| 1 cup, peeled, raw, small diced ½ -inch | = 202g |
| 1 cup, peeled, raw, medium diced ¾-inch | = 180g |
| 1 cup, peeled, raw, large diced 1-inch | = 165g |
| | |
| 1 cup, canned in water pack, tidbits, firmly packed | = 245g |
| 1 cup, canned in juice pack, tidbits, firmly packed | = 250g |
| 1 cup, canned in light syrup, tidbits, firmly packed | = 250g |
| 1 cup, canned in heavy syrup, tidbits, firmly packed | = 255g |
| 1 cup, canned in extra-heavy syrup, tidbits, firmly packed | = 260g |
| | |
| 1 cup, chunks, canned, sweetened | = 247g |
| 1 cup, juice, canned, undiluted, unsweetened | = 250g |
| 1 cup, candied, chopped, firmly packed | = 235g |
| 1 cup, candied, chopped, loosely packed | = 153g |

## PLUM

| | |
|---|---|
| 1 small fruit, whole, raw | =  45g |
| 1 medium fruit, whole, raw | =  60g |
| 1 large fruit, whole, raw | =  90g |
| | |
| 1 cup, pitted, sliced, raw | = 165g |
| 1 cup, canned in water pack, pitted | = 250g |
| 1 cup, canned in juice pack, pitted | = 255g |
| 1 cup, canned in light syrup, pitted | = 255g |
| 1 cup, canned in heavy syrup, pitted | = 260g |
| 1 cup, canned in extra-heavy syrup, pitted | = 265g |

# FRUITS and FRUIT PRODUCTS

**Figure 18.** *Dried, pitted and sweetened prunes*

# FRUITS and FRUIT PRODUCTS

### POMEGRANATE (GRANADA)
    1 cup, arils (seed and juice sacs), raw                              = 174g
    1 cup, juice, sweetened, bottled                                     = 252g

### POMELO
    1 small fruit, *Philippine native*, whole with skin and seeds, raw   = 300g
    1 medium fruit, *Philippine native*, whole with skin and seeds, raw= 1000g
    1 large fruit, *Philippine native*, whole with skin and seeds, raw   = 2000g

    1 small fruit, *Siamese variety*, whole with skin and seeds, raw     = 1000g
    1 medium fruit, *Siamese variety,* whole with skin and seeds, raw    = 1500g
    1 large fruit, *Siamese variety*, whole with skin and seeds, raw     = 2500g

    1 small fruit, *Chinese variety*, whole with skin and seeds, raw     = 600g
    1 medium fruit, *Chinese variety,* whole with skin and seeds, raw    = 1200g
    1 large fruit, *Chinese variety*, whole with skin and seeds, raw     = 1750g

    1 cup, red pulp, sectioned, seeded, raw                              = 205g
    1 cup, red pulp, sectioned, seeded, raw, diced                       = 164g
    1 cup, red pulp, grits, seeded, raw, firmly packed                   = 145g
    1 cup, red pulp, grits, seeded, raw, loosely packed                  =  96g

### PRUNES
    1 small piece dried prune, pitted, uncooked                          =   5g
    1 medium piece dried prune, pitted, uncooked                         =   7g
    1 large piece dried prune, pitted, uncooked                          =   8g
    1 extra-large piece dried prune, pitted, uncooked                    =  10g

    1 cup, dried, with pits, whole, canned                               = 252g
    1 cup, dried, pitted, sweetened, whole, firmly packed                = 185g
    1 cup, dried, pitted, sweetened, chopped, firmly packed              = 233g
    1 cup, dried, pitted, sweetened, chopped, loosely packed             = 137g

# FRUITS and FRUIT PRODUCTS

**PRUNES**

| | |
|---|---|
| 1 cup, stewed, pitted, unsweetened, firmly packed | = 245g |
| 1 cup, stewed, pitted, sweetened, firmly packed | = 255g |
| | |
| 1 cup, juice, canned | = 258g |
| 1 cup, paste, canned | = 320g |
| 1 cup, puree, canned | = 288g |

**RAISINS**

| | |
|---|---|
| 1 cup, with seeds, firmly packed | = 165g |
| 1 cup, with seeds, loosely packed | = 144g |
| | |
| 1 cup, seedless, whole, firmly packed | = 155g |
| 1 cup, seedless, whole, loosely packed | = 137g |
| 1 cup, seedless, whole, rehydrated | = 180g |
| 1 cup, seedless, chopped, firmly packed | = 210g |
| 1 cup, seedless, chopped, loosely packed | = 135g |

**RAMBUTAN**

| | |
|---|---|
| 1 small fruit, with skin and stone | = 33g |
| 1 medium fruit, with skin and stone | = 44g |
| 1 large fruit, with skin and stone | = 67g |
| 1 cup, canned in light syrup, pitted | = 150g |

**RASPBERRIES**

| | |
|---|---|
| 1 cup, whole, raw | = 250g |

**ROSELLE**

| | |
|---|---|
| 1 cup, whole, raw | = 57g |

# FRUITS and FRUIT PRODUCTS

## ROSE APPLE

| | |
|---|---|
| 1 extra-small fruit, whole, raw | = 13g |
| 1 small fruit, whole, raw | = 23g |
| 1 medium fruit, whole, raw | = 43g |
| 1 large fruit, whole, raw | = 63g |
| 1 extra-large fruit, whole, raw | = 83g |
| 1 cup, fruit, extra-small to small, whole, raw | = 122g |
| 1 cup, fruit, halves, raw | = 130g |
| 1 cup, fruit, chopped, raw | = 137g |

## SANTOL, PHILIPPINE NATIVE VARIETY

| | |
|---|---|
| 1 small fruit, whole, with skin and seeds | = 72g |
| 1 medium fruit, whole, with skin and seeds | = 90g |
| 1 large fruit, whole, with skin and seeds | = 125g |

## SANTOL, BANGKOK VARIETY

| | |
|---|---|
| 1 small fruit, whole, with skin and seeds | = 165g |
| 1 medium fruit, whole, with skin and seeds | = 200g |
| 1 large fruit, whole, with skin and seeds | = 330g |

## SAPODILLA (CHICO)

| | |
|---|---|
| 1 extra-small fruit, whole, with skin and seeds | = 40g |
| 1 small fruit, whole, with skin and seeds | = 70g |
| 1 medium fruit, whole, with skin and seeds | = 100g |
| 1 large fruit, whole, with skin and seeds | = 150g |
| 1 extra-large, whole, with skin and seeds | = 200g |
| 1 cup, pulp, no skin and seeds, raw, firmly packed | = 240g |

# FRUITS and FRUIT PRODUCTS

## SAPOTE

| | |
|---|---|
| 1 extra-small fruit, whole with skin seeds, raw | = 200g |
| 1 small fruit, whole with skin and seeds, raw | = 750g |
| 1 medium fruit, whole with skin and seeds, raw | = 1500g |
| 1 large fruit, whole with and seeds, raw | = 2000g |
| 1 extra-large fruit, whole with skin and seeds, raw | = 2500g |
| 1 cup, skinned and seeded, sliced, raw | = 192g |

## SOURSOP

| | |
|---|---|
| 1 extra-small fruit, whole, with skin and seeds | = 250g |
| 1 small fruit, whole, with skin and seeds | = 500g |
| 1 medium fruit, whole, with skin and seeds | = 750g |
| 1 large fruit, whole, with skin and seeds | = 1000g |
| 1 extra-large fruit, whole, with skin and seeds | = 2500g |
| 1 cup, sliced into 2-inch wedge, with skin and seeds, raw | = 140g |
| 1 cup, pulp, no skin and seeds, firmly packed | = 234g |

## SURINAM CHERRY (PITANGA)

| | |
|---|---|
| 1 cup, whole, raw | = 173g |

## SPANISH PLUM

| | |
|---|---|
| 1 small fruit, whole, with skin and stone | = 14g |
| 1 medium fruit, whole, with skin and stone | = 18g |
| 1 large fruit, whole, with skin and stone | = 25g |

## STAR APPLE

| | |
|---|---|
| 1 extra-small fruit, whole, with skin and seeds | = 80g |
| 1 small fruit, whole, with skin and seeds | = 110g |
| 1 medium fruit, whole, with skin and seeds | = 165g |
| 1 large fruit, whole, with skin and seeds | = 330g |

# FRUITS and FRUIT PRODUCTS

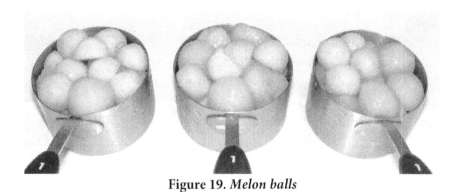

Figure 19. *Melon balls*

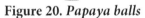

Figure 20. *Papaya balls*

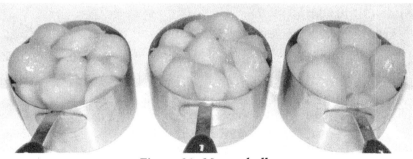

Figure 21. *Mango balls*

# FRUITS and FRUIT PRODUCTS

### STAR APPLE

| | |
|---|---|
| 1 cup, pulp, no skin and seeded, raw, firmly packed | = 245g |
| 1 cup, pulp, no skin and seeded, raw, loosely packed | = 95g |

### STRAWBERRY

| | |
|---|---|
| 1 small fruit, whole, with skin | = 7g |
| 1 medium fruit, whole, with skin | = 12g |
| 1 large fruit, whole, with skin | = 18g |
| 1 extra-large, whole, with skin | = 27g |
| 1 cup, whole, with skin, raw | = 150g |
| 1 cup, halves, with skin, raw | = 160g |
| 1 cup, thinly sliced, raw | = 240g |
| 1 cup, pureed, raw | = 230g |
| 1 cup, stewed, whole, sweetened | = 255g |
| 1 cup, stewed, whole, unsweetened | = 220g |
| 1 cup, stewed, sliced, sweetened | = 266g |
| 1 cup, canned in heavy syrup, whole | = 254g |
| 1 cup, jam, sweetened, bottled | = 320g |

### SUGAR APLE

| | |
|---|---|
| 1 small fruit, whole, with skin and seeds | = 85g |
| 1 medium fruit, whole, with skin and seeds | = 140g |
| 1 large fruit, whole, with skin and seeds | = 200g |
| 1 extra-large fruit, whole, with skin and seeds | = 400g |
| 1 cup, pulp, no skin and seeded, raw, firmly packed | = 270g |
| 1 cup, pulp, no skin and seeded, raw, loosely packed | = 235g |

# FRUITS and FRUIT PRODUCTS

**SUGAR PALM (KAONG)**

| | |
|---|---|
| 1 cup, peeled, uncooked | = 194g |
| 1 cup, bottled in light syrup | = 218g |

**TAMARIND**

| | |
|---|---|
| 1 small fruit, unripe, whole, with skin and seeds | = 25g |
| 1 medium fruit, unripe, whole, with skin and seeds | = 32g |
| 1 large fruit, unripe, whole, with skin and seeds | = 40g |
| 1 cup, unripe, pulp, with seeds, raw | = 132g |
| | |
| 1 small fruit, ripe, whole, with skin and seeds | = 14g |
| 1 medium fruit, ripe, whole, with skin and seeds | = 17g |
| 1 large fruit, ripe, whole, with skin and seeds | = 20g |
| | |
| 1 cup, pulp, ripe, no skin and seeded | = 135g |
| 1 cup, immature fruit, with skin and seeds, boiled | = 175g |
| 1 cup, nectar, canned | = 250g |

# VEGETABLES and VEGETABLE PRODUCTS

# VEGETABLES and VEGETABLE PRODUCTS

### AMARANTH
| | |
|---|---|
| 1 cup, *amaranth* leaves, raw | =  32g |
| 1 cup, *amaranth* leaves, boiled | = 127g |
| 1 cup *spineless amaranth* leaves, raw | =  28g |
| 1 cup *spineless amaranth* leaves, boiled | = 132g |

### ARTICHOKE, GLOBE
| | |
|---|---|
| 1 cup, chopped, raw | = 150g |
| 1 cup, chopped, boiled | = 155g |

### ARUGULA
| | |
|---|---|
| 1 cup, baby arugula, cut into 1 ½ inch long, raw | =  53g |
| 1 cup, aragula leaves, boiled | = 132g |

### ASPARAGUS
| | |
|---|---|
| 1 small spear, 5-inches long, raw | =  12g |
| 1 medium spear, 5 ¼ to 7-inches long, raw | =  16g |
| 1 large spear, 7 ¼ to 8 ½ inches long, raw | =  20g |
| 1 extra-large spear, 8 ¾ to 10 inches long, raw | =  24g |
| | |
| 1 cup, cut into 2-inch long, raw | = 134g |
| 1 spear, boiled, cut into 2-inch long | =  15g |
| 1 cup, cut into 2-inch long, boiled | = 180g |
| 1 cup, canned, drained | = 242g |

### BAMBOO SHOOT
| | |
|---|---|
| 1 cup, chopped, raw | = 140g |
| 1 cup, chopped, boiled | = 135g |
| 1 cup, chopped, stir-fried | = 133g |

# VEGETABLES and VEGETABLE PRODUCTS

## BAMBOO SHOOT

| | |
|---|---|
| 1 cup, cut into strips, raw | = 145g |
| 1 cup, cut into strips, boiled | = 153g |
| 1 cup, cut into strips, stir-fried | = 139g |
| 1 cup, cut into strips, canned, drained | = 130g |

## BANANA BLOSSOM

| | |
|---|---|
| 1 cup, chopped, raw | = 100g |
| 1 cup, chopped, boiled | = 273g |
| | |
| 1 cup, minced, raw, firmly packed | = 169g |
| 1 cup, minced, raw, loosely packed | = 80g |
| 1 cup, minced, boiled, firmly packed | = 191g |
| 1 cup, minced, boiled, loosely packed | = 89g |
| | |
| 1 cup, dried, firmly packed | = 154g |
| 1 cup, dried, loosely packed | = 74g |
| 1 cup, dried, stewed, drained, firmly packed | = 209g |
| 1 cup, dried, stewed, drained, loosely packed | = 104g |

## BEETS

| | |
|---|---|
| 1 cup, root, cut into rounds, raw | = 136g |
| 1 cup, root, cut into rounds, boiled | = 170g |
| 1cup, root, canned, diced, drained | = 157g |
| 1 cup, root, canned, shredded, drained | =195g |
| 1 cup, root, canned, thinly sliced, drained | = 170g |
| | |
| 1 cup, leaves, cut into 1-inch, raw | = 38g |
| 1 cup, leaves, cut into 1-inch, boiled | = 144g |

# VEGETABLES and VEGETABLE PRODUCTS

**Figure 22.** *Dried, stewed, drained, firmly packed banana blossom*

**Figure 23.** *Uncooked, thinly sliced bitter gourd fruit*

# VEGETABLES and VEGETABLE PRODUCTS

## BITTER GOURD

| | |
|---|---|
| 1 small fruit, *long variety*, whole, with seeds, raw | = 100g |
| 1 medium fruit, *long variety*, whole, with seeds, raw | = 200g |
| 1 large fruit, *long variety*, whole, with seeds, raw | = 250g |
| 1 cup fruit, *long variety*, seeded, thinly sliced, raw | = 98g |
| 1 cup fruit, *long variety*, seeded, thinly sliced, boiled | = 120g |
| | |
| 1 small fruit, *round variety*, whole, with seeds, raw | = 65g |
| 1 medium fruit, *round variety*, whole, with seeds, raw | = 80g |
| 1 large fruit, *round variety*, whole, with seeds, raw | = 100g |
| 1 cup, fruit, *round variety*, quartered, seeded, raw | = 98g |
| 1cup, fruit, *round variety*, quartered, seeded, boiled | = 110g |
| | |
| 1 cup, leaves and petioles, raw, loosely packed | = 33g |
| 1 cup, leaves and petioles, boiled, firmly packed | = 144g |

## BLACK NIGHTSHADE

| | |
|---|---|
| 1 cup, leaves, cut into 1 ½ -inch, raw | = 58g |
| 1 cup leaves, cut into 1 ½ -inch, boiled | = 147g |

## BROCCOLI

| | |
|---|---|
| 1 cup, flower, chopped, raw | = 85g |
| 1 cup, flower, chopped, boiled | = 180g |

## CABBAGE

| | |
|---|---|
| 1 cup, *bok choi*, leaves and stem, cut into ½ inch, raw | = 70g |
| 1 cup, *bok choi*, leaves and stem, cut into ½ inch, boiled | = 167g |
| 1 cup, *bok choi*, leaves and stem, cut into 3 inch, raw | = 78g |
| 1 cup, *bok choi*, leaves and stem, cut into 3 inch, boiled | = 180g |
| | |
| 1 cup, *Chinese cabbage*, leaves and stem, cut into ½ inch, raw | = 44g |
| 1 cup, *Chinese cabbage*, leave and stem, cut into ½ inch, boiled | = 160g |

# VEGETABLES and VEGETABLE PRODUCTS

## CABBAGE

| | |
|---|---|
| 1 *green cabbage*, extra-small head  , 4-inch diameter | = 350g |
| 1 *green cabbage*, small head, 4 ½ inch diameter | = 750g |
| 1 *green cabbage*, medium head, 5 ¾ inch diameter | = 1000g |
| 1 *green cabbage*, large head, 7-inch diameter | = 1250g |
| | |
| 1 cup, *green cabbage*, shredded, raw | = 160g |
| 1 cup, *green cabbage*, shredded, boiled | = 168g |
| 1 cup, *green cabbage*, cut into ½-inch, raw | =  80g |
| 1 cup, *green cabbage*, cut into ½-inch, boiled | =  84g |
| | |
| 1 *red cabbage*, small head, 4-inches diameter | = 500g |
| 1 *red cabbage*, medium head, 5-inches diameter | = 900g |
| 1 *red cabbage*, large head, 5 ½ inches diameter | = 1200g |
| | |
| 1 cup, *red cabbage*, thinly shredded, raw | =  86g |
| 1 cup, *red cabbage*, thinly shredded, boiled | = 105g |
| 1 cup, *red cabbage*, cut into ½ inch, raw | =  95g |
| 1 cup, *red cabbage*, cut into ½ inch, boiled | = 105g |
| 1 cup, *red cabbage*, canned, shredded, drained | = 150g |

## CALABASH (LONG VARIETY)

| | |
|---|---|
| 1 extra-small fruit, whole with skin and seeds, raw | = 500g |
| 1 small fruit, whole with skin and seeds, raw | = 1000g |
| 1 medium fruit, whole with skin and seeds, raw | = 2500g |
| 1 large fruit, whole with skin and seeds, raw | = 3500g |
| 1 extra-large fruit, whole with skin and seeds, raw | = 4500g |
| | |
| 1 cup, peeled and seeded, diced into 1-inch, raw | = 140g |
| 1 cup, peeled and seeded, diced into 1-inch, boiled | = 165g |

# VEGETABLES and VEGETABLE PRODUCTS

### CALABASH (ROUND VARIETY)

| | |
|---|---|
| 1 extra-small fruit, whole with skin and seeds, raw | = 700g |
| 1 small fruit, whole with skin and seeds, raw | = 1500g |
| 1 medium fruit, whole with skin and seeds, raw | = 3500g |
| 1 large fruit, whole with skin and seeds, raw | = 5000g |
| 1 extra-large fruit, whole with skin and seeds, raw | = 8000g |

### CAPERS

| | |
|---|---|
| 1 cup, bottled, drained | = 176g |

### CARROTS

| | |
|---|---|
| 1 extra-small tuber, with skin, 5 ½ inches long, raw | = 50g |
| 1 small tuber, with skin, 6 ½ inches long, raw | = 67g |
| 1 medium tuber, with skin 7 ½ inches long, raw | = 100g |
| 1 long tuber, with skin, 8 ½ inches long, raw | = 200g |
| | |
| 1 cup, peeled, diced 1-inch, raw | = 140g |
| 1 cup, peeled, diced ¾ inch, raw | = 143g |
| 1 cup, peeled, diced ½ inch, raw | = 125g |
| | |
| 1 cup, peeled, strips, raw | = 100g |
| 1 cup, peeled, shredded, raw | = 100g |
| 1 cup, peeled, cut into round, ¼ thick, raw | = 110g |
| 1 cup, peeled, cut into wedge, raw | = 113g |
| 1 cup, peeled, minced, firmly packed, raw | = 160g |
| 1 cup, peeled, minced, loosely packed, raw | = 118g |
| | |
| 1 cup, peeled, diced 1 inch, boiled | = 155g |
| 1 cup, peeled, dice ¾ inch, boiled | = 148g |
| 1 cup, peeled, dice ½ inch, boiled | = 182g |

# VEGETABLES and VEGETABLE PRODUCTS

### CARROTS

| | |
|---|---|
| 1 cup, peeled, strips, boiled | = 140g |
| 1 cup, peeled, shredded, boiled | = 141g |
| 1 cup, peeled, cut into round, boiled | = 155g |
| 1 cup, peeled, cut into wedge, boiled | = 155g |
| | |
| 1 cup, peeled, minced, boiled | = 194g |
| 1 cup, peeled, mashed, boiled | = 230g |
| 1 cup, juice, undiluted, canned | = 236g |

### CASSAVA TOPS

| | |
|---|---|
| 1 cup, tops, shredded thinly, raw | = 60g |
| 1 cup, tops, shredded thinly, boiled | = 152g |

### CAULIFLOWER

| | |
|---|---|
| 1 extra-small head, 4 inches diameter, raw | = 250g |
| 1 small head, 5 inches diameter, raw | = 500g |
| 1 medium head, 6 inches diameter, raw | = 1000g |
| 1 large head, raw, 7inches diameter, raw | = 1500g |
| 1 cup florets, raw | = 102g |
| 1 cup florets, boiled | = 128g |

### CELERY

| | |
|---|---|
| 1 stalk, 5 inches long, raw | = 20g |
| 1 stalk, 8 inches long, raw | = 50g |
| 1 stalk, 12 inches long, raw | = 70g |
| 1 cup leaves and petioles, chopped, raw | = 120g |
| 1 cup leaves and petioles, chopped, boiled | = 160g |

### CELERY, CHINESE

| | |
|---|---|
| 1 cup leaves and petioles, cut into 1-inch, raw, loosely packed | = 46g |
| 1 cup leaves and petioles, minced, raw, loosely packed | = 60g |

# VEGETABLES and VEGETABLE PRODUCTS

**Figure 24.** *Boiled, chayote tops*

# VEGETABLES and VEGETABLE PRODUCTS

## CHAYOTE

| | |
|---|---|
| 1 small fruit, whole with skin, raw | = 167g |
| 1 medium fruit, whole with skin, raw | = 250g |
| 1 large fruit, whole with skin, raw | = 500g |
| 1 cup, peeled and seeded fruit, cut into strips 2 x ½ inch, raw | = 135g |
| 1 cup, peeled and seeded fruit, cut into strips 2 x ½ inch, boiled | = 155g |
| 1 cup, chayote tops, raw | = 46g |
| 1 cup, chayote tops, boiled | = 76g |

## COCONUT SHOOT

| | |
|---|---|
| 1 cup, cubed into 1-inch, raw | = 137g |
| 1 cup, cubed into 1-inch, boiled | = 155g |
| 1 cup, cut into strips 2- 2 ½ inch x ½ inch, raw | = 106g |
| 1 cup, cut into strips 2-2 ½ inch x ½ inch, boiled | = 133g |

## COLLARDS

| | |
|---|---|
| 1 cup leaves and stem, chopped, raw | = 33g |
| 1 cup leaves and stem, chopped, boiled | = 121g |
| 1 cup leaves and stem, thinly shredded, raw | = 55g |
| 1 cup leaves and stem, thinly shredded, boiled | = 134g |

## CUCUMBER

| | |
|---|---|
| 1 extra-small fruit, whole, with skin, raw | = 140g |
| 1 small fruit, whole, with skin, raw | = 200g |
| 1 medium fruit, whole, with skin, raw | = 350g |
| 1 large fruit, whole, with skin, raw | = 1000g |
| 1 cup, with skin, thinly sliced, raw | = 100g |
| 1 cup, peeled, thinly sliced, raw | = 120g |
| 1 cup, peeled, cubed into ½ inch, raw | = 142g |
| 1 cup, pickled, cubed into ½ inch | = 160g |
| 1 cup, pickled, minced | = 232g |

# VEGETABLES and VEGETABLE PRODUCTS

**COWPEA**

    1 cup, young pods with seeds, cut into 1-inch long, raw     =   70g

    1 cup, young pods with seeds, cut into 1-inch long, boiled   =   92g

**EGGPLANT**

    1 extra-small fruit, long purple variety, whole, raw     =   33g

    1 small fruit, long purple variety, whole, raw     =   45g

    1 medium fruit long purple variety, whole, raw     =   71g

    1 large fruit, long purple variety, whole, raw     = 167g

    1 extra-small fruit, round purple and green variety, whole, raw =   55g

    1 small fruit, purple and green variety, whole, raw     =   71g

    1 medium fruit, purple and green variety, whole, raw     = 100g

    1 large fruit, purple and green variety, whole, raw     = 170g

    1 cup, wedged, with skin, raw     =   91g

    1 cup, wedged, with skin, boiled     = 171g

    1 cup, cut into rounds ¼ inch thick, with skin, raw     =   74g

    1 cup, cut into rounds ¼ inch thick, with skin, boiled     = 139g

    1 cup, diced into 1 inch, with skin, raw     =   82g

    1 cup, diced into 1 inch with skin, boiled     = 147g

    1 cup, boiled, peeled, mashed     = 223g

    1 cup, pickled     = 136g

**ENDIVE**

    1 cup, leaves and petioles, cut into 1 ½ inch long, raw     =   42g

**FAVA BEANS**

    1 cup, young pods with seeds, cut into 1-inch long, raw     = 130g

    1 cup, young pods with seeds, cut into 1-inch long, boiled   = 143g

# VEGETABLES and VEGETABLE PRODUCTS

**Figure 25.** *Fresh curly endive*

# VEGETABLES and VEGETABLE PRODUCTS

**FERN**

| | |
|---|---|
| 1 cup leaves and petioles, raw | = 28g |
| 1 cup leaves and petioles, boiled | = 68g |

**GARDEN CRESS**

| | |
|---|---|
| 1 cup leaves and petioles, raw | = 50g |
| 1 cup leaves and petioles, boiled | = 135g |

**HORSERADISH**

| | |
|---|---|
| 1 cup leaves with no stem, raw | = 45g |
| 1 cup leaves with no stem, boiled | = 220g |
| 1 cup fruit cut into 2 inches long   , with peel, raw | = 123g |
| 1 cup fruit cut into 2 inches long, with peel, boiled | = 130g |
| 1 cup fruit, cut into 2 inches long, peeled, raw | = 102g |
| 1 cup fruit cut into 2 inches long, peeled, boiled    = | = 112g |

**HYACINTH PODS**

| | |
|---|---|
| 1 cup, immature seeds, raw | = 137g |
| 1 cup, immature seeds, boiled | = 150g |
| 1 cup, young pods with seeds, cut into 1 ½ inch long, raw | = 95g |
| 1 cup, young pods with seeds, cut into 1 ½ inch long, boiled | = 120g |

**JACKFRUIT**

| | |
|---|---|
| 1 cup, unripe fruit, peeled, thinly sliced, raw | = 131g |
| 1 cup, unripe fruit, peeled, thinly sliced, boiled | = 100g |
| 1 cup, jackfruit mature seeds, whole with skin, raw | = 175g |
| 1 cup, jackfruit mature seeds, peeled, boiled, whole | = 180g |
| 1 cup, jackfruit mature seeds, peeled, boiled, chopped | = 149g |

**JUTE**

| | |
|---|---|
| 1 cup leaves, raw | = 34g |
| 1 cup leaves, boiled | = 182g |

# VEGETABLES and VEGETABLE PRODUCTS

**Figure 26.** *Diced, raw, long purple eggplant*

**Figure 27.** *Freshly harvested fern tops*

# VEGETABLES and VEGETABLE PRODUCTS

**Figure 28.** *Hyacinth raw immature seeds*

# VEGETABLES and VEGETABLE PRODUCTS

## KALE
| | |
|---|---|
| 1 cup, leaves and petioles, chopped, raw | = 75g |
| 1 cup, leaves and petioles, chopped, boiled | = 142g |

## KOHLRABI
| | |
|---|---|
| 1 cup, peeled, chopped, raw | = 135g |
| 1 cup, peeled, chopped, boiled | = 165g |

## LEEKS
| | |
|---|---|
| 1 cup bulb and leaves, chopped, raw | = 90g |
| 1 cup bulb and leaves, chopped, boiled | = 120g |

## LETTUCE, BOSTON
| | |
|---|---|
| 1 small leaf, raw | = 5g |
| 1 medium leaf, raw | = 8g |
| 1 large leaf, raw | = 15g |
| 1 head, 5 inches diameter | = 170g |
| 1 cup chopped, raw | = 56g |

## LETTUCE, ICEBERG
| | |
|---|---|
| 1 small leaf, raw | = 5g |
| 1 medium leaf, raw | = 8g |
| 1 large leaf, raw | = 15g |
| 1 small head, whole, raw | = 325g |
| 1 medium head, whole, raw | = 550g |
| 1 large head, whole, raw | = 750g |
| | |
| 1 cup, chopped, raw | = 56g |
| 1 cup, cut into thin strips, raw | = 72g |

# VEGETABLES and VEGETABLE PRODUCTS

**LETTUCE, RED LEAF**

| | |
|---|---|
| 1 small leaf, raw | = 5g |
| 1 medium leaf, raw | = 17g |
| 1 head, whole, raw | = 300g |
| 1 cup, chopped, raw | = 30g |

**LETTUCE, ROMAINE**

| | |
|---|---|
| 1 small leaf, raw | = 6g |
| 1 large leaf, raw | = 28g |
| 1 head, chopped, raw | = 56g |

**LIMA BEAN PODS**

| | |
|---|---|
| 1 cup, immature pod, chopped, raw | = 102g |
| 1 cup, immature pod, chopped, boiled | = 129g |
| 1 cup, immature seeds, raw | = 123g |
| 1 cup, immature seeds, boiled | = 135g |
| 1 cup, immature seeds, canned | = 250g |

**MALABAR SPINACH**

| | |
|---|---|
| 1 cup leaves, raw | = 60g |
| 1 cup leaves, boiled | = 160g |

**MORNING GLORY**

| | |
|---|---|
| 1 cup leaves and petioles, raw | = 46g |
| 1 cup leaves and petioles, boiled | = 135g |

**MUSHROOM, CHAMPIGNON**

| | |
|---|---|
| 1 small piece, whole, raw | = 10g |
| 1 medium piece, whole, raw | = 18g |
| 1 large piece, whole, raw | = 23g |

# VEGETABLES and VEGETABLE PRODUCTS

**Figure 29.** *Morning glory fresh tops*

**Figure 30.** *Boiled morning glory tops*

# VEGETABLES and VEGETABLE PRODUCTS

## MUSHROOM, CHAMPIGNON
| | |
|---|---|
| 1 cup, whole, raw | = 113g |
| 1 cup, thinly sliced, raw | = 90g |
| 1 cup, chopped, raw | = 75g |
| 1 cup, whole, boiled | = 156g |
| | |
| 1 cup, sliced, boiled | = 225g |
| 1 cup, sliced, stir-fried | = 108g |
| 1 cup, canned, whole | = 156g |
| | |
| 1 small piece, canned, whole | = 7g |
| 1 medium piece, canned, whole | = 12g |
| 1 large piece, canned, whole | = 16g |

## MUSHROOM, CHANTERRELE
| | |
|---|---|
| 1 piece mushroom, whole, raw | = 5g |
| 1 cup, whole, raw | = 54g |

## MUSHROOM, CLOUD EAR
| | |
|---|---|
| 1 cup, whole, raw | = 76g |
| 1 cup, whole, boiled | = 96g |
| 1 cup, shredded, raw | = 106g |
| 1 cup, shredded, boiled | = 126g |

## MUSHROOM, COMMON SPLIT-GILL (KURAKDING)
| | |
|---|---|
| 1 cup, whole, raw | = 52g |
| 1 cup, whole, boiled | = 75g |

## MUSHROOM, ENOKI
| | |
|---|---|
| 1 medium piece enoki mushroom, raw | = 3g |
| 1 large piece enoki mushroom, raw | = 5g |
| 1 cup, enoki mushroom, raw | = 65g |

# VEGETABLES and VEGETABLE PRODUCTS

Figure 31. *Fresh whole cloud ear mushroom*

# VEGETABLES and VEGETABLE PRODUCTS

## MUSHROOM, OYSTER

| | |
|---|---|
| 1 piece oyster mushroom, whole, raw | = 15g |
| 1 cup, whole, raw | = 86g |
| 1 cup, shredded, raw | = 76g |
| 1 cup, shredded, boiled | = 98g |

## MUSHROOM, PORTABELLA

| | |
|---|---|
| 1 cup, sliced, raw | = 84g |
| 1 cup, sliced grilled | = 121g |

## MUSHROOM, SHIITAKE

| | |
|---|---|
| 1 piece, whole, fresh | = 19g |
| 1 piece, whole, dried | = 4g |
| 1 piece, whole, boiled | = 18g |
| 1 piece, whole, stir-fried | = 19g. |
| | |
| 1 cup, whole, boiled | = 145g |
| 1 cup, whole stir-fried | = 89g |
| 1 cup, sliced, stir-fried | = 97g |

## MUSTARD GREENS

| | |
|---|---|
| 1 cup, leaves, cut into 2 inches long, raw | = 65g |
| 1 cup, leaves, cut into 2 inches long, boiled | = 145g |

## NEW ZEALAND SPINACH

| | |
|---|---|
| 1 cup, leaves, raw | = 56g |
| 1 cup, leaves, boiled | = 180g |

## OKRA

| | |
|---|---|
| 1 small pod, whole, raw | = 25g |
| 1 medium pod, whole, raw | = 40g |
| 1 large pod, whole raw | = 70g |

# VEGETABLES and VEGETABLE PRODUCTS

## OKRA

| | |
|---|---|
| 1 cup pod, cut into 2 inches long, raw | = 94g |
| 1 cup pod, cut into 2 inches long, boiled | = 126g |
| 1 cup pod, cut into ½ inch, raw | = 120g |
| 1 cup pod, cut into ½ inch, boiled | = 175g |
| 1 piece pod, whole, boiled | = 12g |

## PAPAYA FRUIT

| | |
|---|---|
| 1 cup, unripe fruit, peeled, seeded, cut 1-inch diagonally, raw | = 140g |
| 1 cup, unripe fruit, peeled, seeded, cut 1-inch diagonally, boiled | = 162g |
| 1 cup, unripe fruit, peeled, seeded, cut into thin strips, raw | = 153g |
| 1 cup, unripe fruit, peeled, seeded, cut into thin strips, boiled | = 175g |
| 1 cup, unripe fruit, peeled and seeded, grated, raw, firmly packed | = 180g |
| 1 cup, unripe fruit, peeled and seeded, grated, raw, loosely packed | = 103g |

## PARSNIP

| | |
|---|---|
| 1 cup, peeled, medium diced, raw | = 140g |
| 1 cup, peeled, medium diced, boiled | = 170g |

## PECHAY

| | |
|---|---|
| 1 cup leaves and petioles, cut into 3 inches diameter, raw | = 77g |
| 1 cup leaves and petioles, cut into 3 inches diameter, boiled | = 169g |
| 1 cup leaves and petioles, cut into ½ inch diameter, raw | = 59g |
| 1 cup leaves and petioles, cut into ½ inch diameter, boiled | = 137g |

## PEPPER, CHILI

| | |
|---|---|
| 1 cup leaves, raw | = 21g |
| 1 cup leaves, boiled | = 147g |
| 1 cup, fruit, red and green, chopped, raw | = 150g |

# VEGETABLES and VEGETABLE PRODUCTS

### PEPPER, GREEN FINGER (LONG VARIETY)

| | |
|---|---|
| 1 small fruit, whole, raw | = 10g |
| 1 medium fruit, whole, raw | = 20g |
| 1 large fruit, whole, raw | = 30g |
| 1 cup, cut into ½ inch, raw | = 98g |
| 1 cup, cut into ½ inch, boiled | = 109g |

### PEPPER, JALAPENO

| | |
|---|---|
| 1 cup, fruit, sliced into ½-inch, raw | = 95g |
| 1 cup, fruit, sliced into ½-inch, boiled | = 106g |

### PEPPER, SWEET RED, YELLOW and GREEN

| | |
|---|---|
| 1 small fruit, whole, raw | = 30g |
| 1 medium fruit, whole, raw | = 75g |
| 1 large fruit, whole, raw | = 120g |
| 1 extra-large, whole, raw | = 200g |
| | |
| 1 cup seeded, cut into strips, raw | = 100g |
| 1 cup, seeded, diced into 1 inch, raw | = 129g |
| 1 cup, seeded, diced into ½ inch, raw | = 143g |
| | |
| 1 cup, seeded, cut into strips, sautéed | = 120g |
| 1 cup, seeded, diced into 1 inch, boiled | = 139g |
| 1 cup, seeded, diced into ½ inch, boiled | = 155g |

### PIGEON PEAS

| | |
|---|---|
| 1 cup, immature pod, cut into 1-inch, raw | = 92g |
| 1 cup, immature pod, cut into 1-inch, boiled | = 114g |
| 1 cup, immature seeds, fresh, raw | = 160g |
| 1 cup, immature seeds, fresh, boiled | = 177g |

# VEGETABLES and VEGETABLE PRODUCTS

**PURSLANE**

| | |
|---|---|
| 1 cup leaves and stem, raw | = 43g |
| 1 cup leaves and stem, boiled | = 115g |

**RADICCHIO**

| | |
|---|---|
| 1 small head, whole, raw | = 85g |
| 1 medium head, whole, raw | = 125g |
| 1 large head, whole, raw | = 175g |
| 1 cup, shredded, raw | = 40g |

**RADISH**

| | |
|---|---|
| 1 small tuber, whole, with skin, raw | = 100g |
| 1 medium tuber, whole, with skin, raw | = 125g |
| 1 large tuber, whole, with skin, raw | = 175g |
| 1 extra-large tuber, whole, with skin, raw | = 250g |
| 1 cup, peeled, thinly sliced, raw | = 120g |
| 1 cup, peeled, thinly sliced, boiled | = 150g |
| 1 cup, peeled, thinly sliced, dried | = 127g |

**RHUBARB**

| | |
|---|---|
| 1 piece stalk, raw | = 51g |
| 1 cup, diced, raw | = 122g |
| 1 cup, diced, stewed, sweetened | = 252g |

**RUTABAGAS**

| | |
|---|---|
| 1 small tuber, whole, raw | = 192g |
| 1 medium tuber, whole, raw | = 386g |
| 1 large tuber, whole, raw | = 772g |
| 1 cup, peeled, cubed, raw | = 140g |
| 1 cup, peeled, cubed, boiled | = 170g |
| 1 cup, boiled, mashed | = 240g |

# VEGETABLES and VEGETABLE PRODUCTS

**Figure 32.** *Seeded and diced green bell pepper*

# VEGETABLES and VEGETABLE PRODUCTS

## SALSIFY
 1 cup, peeled, sliced, raw       = 133g
 1 cup, peeled, sliced, boiled      = 135g

## SEAWEED
 1 cup, *lato*, large variety, fresh, raw    = 101g
 1 cup, *lato*, small variety, fresh, raw    = 106g
 1 cup, *guso*, fresh, raw       =  68g
 1 cup, *guso,* boiled        = 148g

 1 cup, *kawkawayan*, fresh, raw     =  54g
 1 cup, *kawkawayan,* boiled      = 206g
 1 cup, *spirulina*, dried, flaked     = 112g
 1 cup, seaweed, dried, seasoned, flaked   =  25g

## SESAME LEAVES (PERILLA)
 1 cup, leaves and petioles, cut into 3-inches, raw   =  56g
 1 cup, leaves and petioles, cut into 3-inches, boiled   = 167g

## SESBANIA
 1 piece flower, raw        =   3g
 1 cup flower, raw         =  20g
 1 cup flower, boiled        = 104g

## SNAP BEANS
 1 cup, immature green pod, sliced into 2-inch, raw   = 106g
 1 cup, immature green pod, sliced into 2-inch, boiled   = 120g
 1 cup, immature green pod, sliced into 1-inch, raw   = 102g
 1 cup, immature green pod, sliced into 1-inch, boiled   = 110g

# VEGETABLES and VEGETABLE PRODUCTS

**Figure 33.** *Fresh guso seaweed*

# VEGETABLES and VEGETABLE PRODUCTS

### SNAP BEANS

| | |
|---|---|
| 1 cup, immature green pod, sliced into ¼-inch, raw | = 110g |
| 1 cup, immature green pod, sliced into ¼-inch, boiled | = 127g |
| 1 cup, green pods, canned, drained | = 240g |
| | |
| 1 cup, immature yellow pod, sliced into ¼-inch, raw | = 107g |
| 1 cup, immature yellow pod, sliced into ¼-inch, boiled | = 120g |
| 1 cup, yellow pods, canned, drained | = 240g |

### SNOW PEAS POD

| | |
|---|---|
| 1 cup, immature pod, whole, raw | = 70g |
| 1 cup, immature pod, whole, boiled | = 85g |
| 1 cup, immature pod, chopped, raw | = 100g |
| 1 cup, immature pod, chopped, boiled | = 119g |

### SPINACH

| | |
|---|---|
| 1 cup, baby leaves with petioles, raw | = 42g |
| 1 cup, baby leaves with petioles, boiled | = 143g |
| 1 cup, leaves with petioles, raw | = 56g |
| 1 cup leaves with petioles, boiled | = 224g |

### SPONGE GOURD

| | |
|---|---|
| 1 small fruit, whole, with skin and seeds, raw | = 125g |
| 1 medium fruit, whole, with skin and seeds, raw | = 250g |
| 1 large fruit, whole, with skin and seeds, raw | = 500g |
| | |
| 1 cup, peeled, sliced into rounds, raw | = 100g |
| 1 cup, peeled, sliced into rounds, boiled | = 178g |
| 1 cup, peeled, diced into 1 ½ inch, raw | = 105g |
| 1 cup, peeled, diced into 1 ½ inch, boiled | = 187g |

# VEGETABLES and VEGETABLE PRODUCTS

**Figure 34.** *Dried, flaked, seasoned seaweed*

# VEGETABLES and VEGETABLE PRODUCTS

## SQUASH FLOWER

| | | |
|---|---|---|
| 1 small piece flower, raw | = | 3g |
| 1 cup small size flower, raw | = | 56g |
| 1 cup small size flower, boiled | = | 162g |
| | | |
| 1 large piece flower, raw | = | 5g |
| 1 cup large size flower, raw | = | 36g |
| 1 cup large size flower, boiled | = | 142g |

## SQUASH FRUIT (OBLONG VARIETY)

| | |
|---|---|
| 1 small fruit, whole with skin and seeds, raw | = 1500g |
| 1 medium fruit, whole with skin and seeds, raw | = 2500g |
| 1 large fruit, whole with skin and seeds, raw | = 3500g |

## SQUASH FRUIT (ROUND VARIETY)

| | |
|---|---|
| 1 extra-small fruit, whole with skin and seeds, raw | = 750g |
| 1 small fruit, whole with skin and seeds, raw | = 1000g |
| 1 medium fruit, whole with skin and seeds, raw | = 2500g |
| 1 large fruit, whole with skin and seeds, raw | = 3500g |
| 1 extra-large fruit, whole with skin and seeds, raw | = 6000g |
| | |
| 1 cup, peeled and seeded cut into 2 inches, raw | = 140g |
| 1 cup, peeled and seeded cut into 2 inches, boiled | = 160g |
| 1 cup, peeled and seeded cut into 1 inch, raw | = 150g |
| 1 cup, peeled and seeded cut into 1 inch, boiled | = 175g |
| 1 cup, peeled and seeded, boiled, mashed | = 248g |

## STRING BEANS

| | |
|---|---|
| 1 cup, immature pods, cut into 2 ½ inch long, raw | = 122g |
| 1 cup, immature pods, cut into 2 ½ inch long, boiled | = 139g |

# VEGETABLES and VEGETABLE PRODUCTS

## SWEET POTATO LEAVES
| | |
|---|---|
| 1 cup leaves and petioles, raw | = 38g |
| 1 cup leaves and petioles, boiled | = 106g |

## SWISS CHARD
| | |
|---|---|
| 1 cup, chopped, raw | = 36g |
| 1 cup, chopped, boiled | = 175g |

## TARO
| | |
|---|---|
| 1 cup taro leaves, shredded, fresh, raw | = 33g |
| 1 cup taro leaves, shredded, fresh, boiled | = 126g |
| | |
| 1 cup, taro stem, cut into 2-inch long, raw | = 88g |
| 1 cup, taro stem, cut into 2-inch long, boiled | = 115g |
| 1 cup, taro stem, cut into ¼ inch, raw | = 94g |
| 1 cup, taro stem, cut into ¼ inch, raw | = 141g |
| | |
| 1 cup taro leaves, shredded, dried, raw | = 35g |
| 1 cup taro leaves, shredded, dried, boiled | = 150g |
| 1 cup taro leaves and stem, chopped, dried, raw | = 35g |
| 1 cup taro leaves and stem, chopped, dried, boiled | = 184g |
| 1 cup taro shoots, chopped, raw | = 86g |
| 1 cup taro shoots, chopped, boiled | = 140g |

## TOMATO
| | |
|---|---|
| 1 fruit, *cherry*, whole, raw | = 17g |
| 1 cup, *cherry*, whole, raw | = 150g |
| | |
| 1 small fruit, *green*, whole raw | = 90g |
| 1 medium fruit, *green*, whole, raw | = 125g |
| 1 large fruit, *green*, whole, raw | = 180g |
| 1 cup, *green*, sliced, raw | = 180g |

# VEGETABLES and VEGETABLE PRODUCTS

**Figure 35.** *Dried taro leaves and stalks*

**Figure 36.** *Boiled dried taro leaves and stalks*

# VEGETABLES and VEGETABLE PRODUCTS

## TOMATO, RED

| | |
|---|---|
| 1 extra-small fruit, *red*, whole, raw | = 12g |
| 1 small fruit, *red*, whole, raw | = 30g |
| 1 medium fruit, *red*, whole, raw | = 75g |
| 1 large fruit, *red*, whole, raw | = 125g |
| 1 extra-large fruit, *red*, whole, raw | = 165g |
| | |
| 1 cup, red tomato, with peel, sliced, raw | = 160g |
| 1 cup, red tomato, with peel, sliced, boiled | = 252g |
| 1 cup, red tomato, with peel, crushed, canned | = 242g |
| 1 cup, red tomato, sun-dried | = 54g |
| | |
| 1 cup, tomato sauce, canned | = 245g |
| 1 cup, tomato paste, canned | = 262g |
| 1 cup, tomato catsup, bottled | = 240g |
| | |
| 1 cup, tomato juice, bottled | = 243g |
| 1 cup, tomato puree, canned | = 250g |
| 1 cup, tomato seed oil, bottled | = 218g |

## TURNIPS

| | |
|---|---|
| 1 medium tuber, whole with skin, raw | = 125g |
| 1 large tuber, whole with skin, raw | = 200g |
| 1 cup, peeled, diced into 1 inch, raw | = 130g |
| 1 cup, peeled, diced into 1 inch, boiled | = 156g |
| 1 cup, peeled, thinly sliced, raw | = 227g |
| 1 cup, peeled, boiled, mashed | = 230g |

## TURNIP, GREENS

| | |
|---|---|
| 1 cup leaves, chopped, raw | = 55g |
| 1 cup leaves, chopped, boiled | = 163g |

# VEGETABLES and VEGETABLE PRODUCTS

### WATER CHESTNUTS (CHINESE)
| | | |
|---|---|---|
| 1 piece, whole raw | = | 9g |
| 1 cup, whole, raw | = | 124g |
| 1 cup, canned, sliced, drained | = | 140g |

### WATER CRESS
| | | |
|---|---|---|
| 1 cup, leaves and petioles, raw | = | 39g |
| 1 cup, leaves and petioles, boiled | = | 151g |

### WATER SPINACH (SWAMP CABBAGE)
| | | |
|---|---|---|
| 1 cup, leaves and stem, cut into 2-inch long, raw | = | 43g |
| 1 cup, leaves and stem, cut into 2-inch long, boiled | = | 139g |
| 1 cup, stem only, cut into 2-inch long, boiled | = | 59g |
| 1 cup, stem only, cut into 2-inch long, boiled | = | 70g |

### WAXGOURD
| | | |
|---|---|---|
| 1 extra-small fruit, whole with skin and seeds, raw | = | 500g |
| 1 small fruit, whole with skin and seeds, raw | = | 1500g |
| 1 medium fruit, whole with skin and seeds, raw | = | 2500g |
| 1 large fruit, whole with skin and seeds, raw | = | 4000g |
| 1 extra-large fruit, whole with skin and seeds, raw | = | 5000g |
| | | |
| 1 cup, peeled and seeded, raw | = | 148g |
| 1 cup, peeled and seeded, boiled | = | 175g |

### WINGED BEANS PODS
| | | |
|---|---|---|
| 1 cup, immature pods, cut into 2-inch long, raw | = | 66g |
| 1 cup, immature pods, cut into 2-inch long, boiled | = | 87g |
| 1 cup, immature pods, thinly sliced, raw | = | 57g |
| 1 cup, immature pods, thinly sliced, boiled | = | 80g |

# VEGETABLES and VEGETABLE PRODUCTS

**Figure 37.** *Cuts of immature winged bean pods*

# VEGETABLES and VEGETABLE PRODUCTS

### YAMBEAN (JICAMA)

| | |
|---|---|
| 1 extra-small tuber, whole with skin, raw | = 100g |
| 1 small tuber, whole with skin, raw | = 125g |
| 1 medium tuber, whole with skin, raw | = 165g |
| 1 large tuber, whole with skin, raw | = 250g |
| 1 extra-large tuber, whole with skin, raw | = 500g |
| | |
| 1 cup, peeled, diced into 1 inch, raw | = 130g |
| 1 cup, peeled, diced into 1 inch, boiled | = 156g |
| 1 cup, peeled cut into strips, raw, firmly packed | = 130g |
| 1 cup, peeled, cut into strips, raw, loosely packed | = 100g |

### ZUCCHINI

| | |
|---|---|
| 1 small fruit, whole with skin, raw | = 125g |
| 1 medium fruit, whole with skin, raw | = 200g |
| 1 large fruit, whole with skin, raw | = 350g |
| | |
| 1 cup, with skin, cut into rounds ½-inch thick, raw | = 127g |
| 1 cup, with skin, cut into rounds ½-inch thick, boiled | = 196g |
| 1 cup, with skin, diced into1-inch, raw | = 143g |
| 1 cup, with skin, diced into 1-inch, raw | = 205g |

# HERBS and SPICES

# HERBS and SPICES

| | |
|---|---|
| 1 cup, *allspice*, ground, firmly packed | = 142g |
| 1 cup, *allspice*, ground, loosely packed | = 107g |
| 1 cup, *anise seeds*, whole, dried | = 107g |
| 1 cup, *anise seeds*, ground | = 70g |
| 1 cup, *annatto seeds*, whole, dried | = 160g |
| 1 cup, *annatto seeds*, ground | = 162g |
| | |
| 1 cup, *basil*, whole leaves, fresh | = 35g |
| 1 cup, *basil*, chopped leaves, fresh | = 42g |
| 1 cup, *basil*, whole leaves, dried | = 65g |
| 1 cup, *basil*, ground, dried | = 72g |
| 1 cup, *bay leaf*, dried, crumpled | = 70g |
| | |
| 1 cup, *borage*, cut into 1-inch, raw | = 89g |
| 1 cup, *caraway*, dried seeds | = 110g |
| 1 cup, *cardamom*, dried seeds | = 95g |
| 1 cup, *celery*, dried seeds | = 101g |
| 1 cup, *chervil*, dried leaves | = 30g |
| | |
| 1 cup, *chicory greens*, chopped, raw | = 29g |
| 1 cup, *chives*, chopped, raw | = 48g |
| 1 cup, *chili* paste | = 285g |
| 1 cup, *chili* powder | = 119g |
| 1 cup, *chives*, fresh, chopped | = 37g |
| 1 cup, *cilantro*, fresh, chopped | = 20g |
| | |
| 1 cup, *cinnamon*, ground | = 108g |
| 1 cup, *coriander seeds*, dried, whole | = 72g |
| 1 cup, *coriander seeds*, ground | = 80g |
| 1 cup, *cumin*, dried seeds | = 100g |
| 1 cup, *curry powder*, loosely packed | = 100g |

# HERBS and SPICES

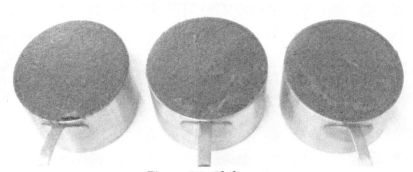

Figure 38. *Chili paste*

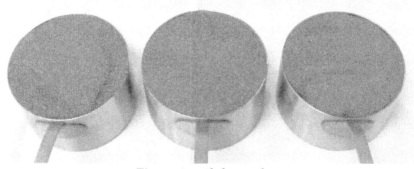

Figure 39. *Chili powder*

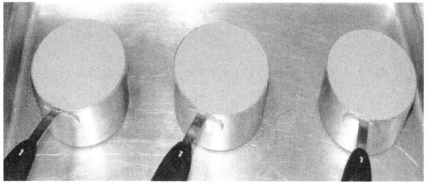

Figure 40. *Curry powder*

# HERBS and SPICES

| | |
|---|---|
| 1 cup, *dill*, weed, fresh | = 10g |
| 1 cup, *dill*, weed, dried | = 50g |
| 1 cup, *dill*, seeds, dried | = 110g |
| | |
| 1 cup, *fennel*, seeds, dried | = 90g |
| 1 cup, *fennel*, bulb, thinly sliced, raw | = 87g |
| 1 cup, *fenugreek*, seeds, dried | = 178g |
| | |
| 1 small bulb, *garlic*, whole, raw | = 10g |
| 1 medium bulb, *garlic*, whole, raw | = 15g |
| 1 large bulb, *garlic*, whole, raw | = 30g |
| 1 piece clove, *garlic*, raw | = 3g |
| | |
| 1 cup, *garlic*, peeled, whole, raw, large variety | = 203g |
| 1 cup, *garlic*, peeled, whole, raw, small variety | = 140g |
| 1 cup, *garlic*, peeled, minced, raw | = 123g |
| 1 cup, *garlic*, peeled, minced, fried | = 162g |
| 1 cup, *garlic*, peeled, cut into round, raw | = 126g |
| 1 cup, *garlic*, peeled, cut into sticks, raw | = 98g |
| | |
| 1 cup, *garlic*, powdered, firmly packed | = 143g |
| 1 cup, *garlic*, powdered, loosely packed | = 108g |
| 1 cup, *garlic*, powdered with salt, firmly packed | = 250g |
| | |
| 1 cup, *ginger root*, peeled, thinly cut, 1-inch diameter, raw | = 145g |
| 1 cup, *ginger root*, peeled, cut into strips, raw | = 105g |
| 1 cup, *ginger root*, peeled, grated, firmly packed, raw | = 144g |
| 1 cup, *ginger root*, peeled, grated, loosely packed, raw | = 88g |
| 1 cup, *ginger root*, dried, ground | = 87g |
| | |
| 1 cup, *lemon grass*, chopped, raw | = 67g |
| 1 cup, *mace*, dried, ground | = 85g |

# HERBS and SPICES

**Figure 41.** *Dried, whole coriander seeds*

**Figure 42.** *Dried parsley flakes*

**Figure 43.** *Fresh rosemary leaves*

# HERBS and SPICES

| | | |
|---|---|---|
| 1 cup, *marjoram*, leaves, fresh, raw, firmly packed | = | 60g |
| 1 cup, *marjoram*, leaves, fresh, raw, loosely packed | = | 25g |
| 1 cup, *marjoram*, leaves, fresh, boiled, drained | = | 120g |
| 1 cup, *marjoram*, leaves, dried, ground | = | 27g |
| | | |
| 1 cup, *mint leaves*, fresh, raw, firmly packed | = | 50g |
| 1 cup, *mint leaves*, fresh, raw, loosely packed | = | 20g |
| 1 cup, *mint leaves*, fresh, boiled | = | 127g |
| 1 cup, *mustard seed*, ground | = | 187g |
| 1 cup, *nutmeg*, ground | = | 110g |
| | | |
| 1 cup, *olive, green*, bottled, cut into rings | = | 126g |
| 1 cup, *olive, green*, bottled, pitted | = | 138g |
| 1 cup, *olive, black*, bottled, cut into rings | = | 128g |
| 1 cup, *olive, black*, bottled, pitted | = | 140g |
| 1 cup, *olive, green*, bottled, cut into rings | = | 126g |
| 1 cup, *olive green*, bottled, pitted | = | 138g |

## ONION

| | | |
|---|---|---|
| 1 small bulb, *onion, Bermuda variety (white)*, raw | = | 50g |
| 1 medium bulb, *onion, Bermuda variety (white)*, raw | = | 70g |
| 1 large bulb, *onion, Bermuda variety (white)*, raw | = | 125g |
| | | |
| 1 small bulb, *onion, Red Globe variety*, raw | = | 50g |
| 1 medium bulb, *onion, Red Globe variety*, raw | = | 100g |
| 1 large bulb, *onion*, Red *Globe variety*, raw | = | 150g |
| | | |
| 1 cup, *onion*, spring, thinly sliced tops and bulb, raw | = | 100g |
| 1 cup, *onion*, spring, thinly sliced tops only | = | 53g |
| 1 cup, *onion*, peeled, white, chopped, raw | = | 158g |
| 1 cup, *onion*, peeled, white, chopped, boiled | = | 209g |

# HERBS and SPICES

## ONION

| | |
|---|---|
| 1 cup, *onion*, peeled, red, minced, raw | = 115g |
| 1 cup, *onion*, peeled, red, cut into rings, raw | = 140g |
| 1 cup, *onion*, peeled, red, chopped, oil-roasted | = 76g |
| 1 cup, *onion*, powdered, firmly packed | = 133g |
| 1 cup, *onion*, powdered, loosely packed | = 105g |
| | |
| 1 cup, *oregano*, leaves, dried, whole | = 50g |
| 1 cup, *oregano*, leaves, dried, ground | = 86g |
| 1 cup, *pandan*, leaves cut into 2-inch long, fresh, raw | = 40g |
| 1 cup, *paprika*, ground | = 108g |
| | |
| 1 cup, *parsley*, leaves, fresh, coarsely chopped | = 28g |
| 1 cup, *parsley* leaves, dried, ground | = 22g |
| 1 cup, *parsley* leaves, dried, flaked | = 25g |
| 1 cup, *pepper jalapeño*, fresh, sliced, raw | = 90g |
| 1 cup, *pepper jalapeño*, canned, sliced | = 143g |
| | |
| 1 cup, *peppercorn*, black, whole, dried | = 113g |
| 1 cup, *peppercorn*, black, whole, coarsely ground | = 100g |
| 1 cup, *peppercorn*, black, ground | = 105g |
| 1 cup, *peppercorn*, white, ground | = 153g |
| 1 cup, *peppercorn*, red, ground | = 86g |
| | |
| 1 cup, *pimiento*, canned, whole, drained | = 190g |
| 1 cup, *pimiento*, canned, coarsely chopped, firmly packed | = 198g |
| 1 cup, *rosemary*, leaves, fresh, whole | = 27g |
| 1 cup, *rosemary*, leaves, dried, whole | = 53g |
| | |
| 1 cup, *safflower*, dried | = 104g |
| 1 cup, *saffron*, dried, loosely packed | = 35g |
| 1 cup, *savory*, ground | = 74g |

# HERBS and SPICES

| | |
|---|---|
| 1 cup, *shallots*, fresh, minced, freshly packed | = 175g |
| 1 cup, *shallots*, fresh, minced, loosely packed | = 160g |
| 1 cup, *spearmint,* leaves, fresh | = 90g |
| 1 cup, *spearmint,* leaves, dried, whole | = 22g |
| | |
| 1 cup, *star anise*, dried | = 85g |
| 1 cup, *sweet basil*, leaves, fresh, thinly sliced | = 80g |
| 1 cup, *sweet basil*, leaves, fresh, whole | = 50g |
| | |
| 1 cup, *tarragon*, leaves, fresh, whole, firmly packed | = 58g |
| 1 cup, *tarragon*, leaves, fresh, whole, loosely packed | = 29g |
| 1 cup, *tarragon*, leaves, fresh, whole, boiled, drained | = 78g |
| 1 cup, *tarragon*, leaves, dried, ground | = 80g |
| | |
| 1 cup, *thyme*, leaves, fresh | = 37g |
| 1 cup, *thyme*, leaves, dried, ground | = 68g |
| | |
| 1 cup, *turmeric*, peeled, finely chopped, firmly packed | = 126g |
| 1 cup, *turmeric*, peeled, finely chopped, loosely packed | = 98g |
| 1 cup, *turmeric*, peeled, cut into strips, firmly packed | = 92g |
| 1 cup, *turmeric*, peeled, cut into strips, loosely packed | = 75g |
| 1 cup, *turmeric*, dried, ground | = 108g |
| | |
| 1 cup, *wasabi root*, peeled, thinly sliced, raw | = 130g |

# LEGUMES, NUTS, SEEDS and PRODUTS

# LEGUMES, NUTS, SEEDS and PRODUCTS

## BEANS

| | |
|---|---|
| 1 cup, *adzuki*, mature seeds, raw | = 197g |
| 1 cup, *adzuki*, mature seeds, boiled | = 230g |
| 1 cup, *adzuki*, mature seeds, canned, sweetened | = 296g |
| | |
| 1 cup, *black*, mature seeds, raw | = 194g |
| 1 cup, *black*, mature seeds, boiled | = 172g |
| 1 cup, *black*, mature seeds, canned, salted | = 184g |
| | |
| 1 cup, *black turtle*, mature seeds, raw | = 184g |
| 1 cup, *black turtle*, mature seeds, boiled | = 185g |
| 1 cup, *black turtle*, mature seeds, canned | = 240g |
| | |
| 1 cup, cannellini, mature seeds, raw | = 215g |
| 1 cup, cannellini, mature seeds, boiled | = 190g |
| | |
| 1 cup, *fava*, mature seeds, raw | = 150g |
| 1 cup, *fava*, mature seeds, boiled | = 170g |
| 1 cup, *fava*, mature seeds, canned, drained | = 256g |
| | |
| 1 cup, *hyacinth*, mature seeds, raw | = 210g |
| 1 cup, *hyacinth*, mature seeds, boiled | = 195g |
| | |
| 1 cup, *kidney red*, mature seeds, raw | = 180g |
| 1 cup, *kidney red*, mature seeds, boiled | = 172g |
| 1 cup, *kidney red*, matured seeds, canned | = 260g |
| 1 cup, *kidney red*, mature seeds, sprouted, raw | = 186g |
| | |
| 1 cup, *lima*, mature seeds, raw | = 170g |
| 1 cup, *lima*, mature seeds, boiled | = 182g |

# LEGUMES, NUTS, SEEDS and PRODUCTS

Figure 44. *Boiled, unsweetened adzuki beans*

Figure 45. *Boiled sweetened adzuki beans*

Figure 46. *Yellow, uncooked mung beans*

# LEGUMES, NUTS, SEEDS and PRODUCTS

**Figure 47.** *Boiled red kidney beans*

**Figure 48.** *Boiled cannellini beans*

# LEGUMES, NUTS, SEEDS and PRODUCTS

## BEANS

| | |
|---|---|
| 1 cup, *mung bean*, mature seeds, green, whole, raw | = 190g |
| 1 cup, *mung bean*, mature seeds, green, crushed, raw | = 178g |
| 1 cup, *mung bean*, mature seeds, yellow, whole, raw | = 192g |
| | |
| 1 cup, *mung bean*, mature seeds, green, whole, raw | = 190g |
| 1 cup, *mung bean*, mature seeds, green, crushed, raw | = 178g |
| 1 cup, *mung bean*, mature seeds, yellow, whole, raw | = 192g |
| | |
| 1 cup, *mung bean*, mature seeds, green, boiled | = 160g |
| 1 cup, *mung bean*, mature seeds, sprout, short tail, raw | = 126g |
| 1 cup, *mung bean*, mature seed, sprout, short tail, boiled | = 150g |
| | |
| 1 cup, *mung bean*, mature seeds, sprout, long tail, raw, firmly packed | = 100g |
| 1 cup, *mung bean*, mature seeds, sprout, long tail, raw, loosely packed | = 70g |
| 1 cup, *mung bean*, mature seeds, sprout, long tail, stir-fried | = 125g |
| | |
| 1 cup, *navy*, mature seeds, raw | = 193g |
| 1 cup, *navy*, mature seeds, boiled | = 168g |
| 1 cup, *navy*, mature seeds, canned | = 240g |
| 1 cup, *navy*, matured seeds, sprouted, raw | = 100g |
| | |
| 1 cup, *pinto*, mature seeds, raw | = 193g |
| 1 cup, *pinto*, mature seeds, boiled | = 175g |
| 1 cup, *pinto*, matured seeds, canned | = 240g |
| | |
| 1 cup, *soy*, mature seeds, raw | = 190g |
| 1 cup, *soy*, mature seeds, boiled | = 172g |
| 1 cup, *soy*, mature seeds, dry roasted | = 95g |
| 1 cup, *soy*, mature seeds, sprouted, raw | = 70g |

# LEGUMES, NUTS, SEEDS and PRODUCTS

## BEANS

| | |
|---|---|
| 1 cup, *soy* flour, stirred | = 84g |
| 1 cup, *soy* milk | = 243g |
| 1 cup, *soy* miso | = 275g |
| 1 cup, *soy* natto | = 175g |
| 1 cup, *soy* taho | = 220g |
| 1 cup, *soy* tempeh | = 166g |
| 1 cup, *soy*, tokwa, cubed, uncooked | = 120g |
| | |
| 1 cup, *winged*, mature seeds, raw | = 182g |
| 1 cup, *winged*, mature seeds, boiled | = 172g |

## LENTILS

| | |
|---|---|
| 1 cup, mature seeds, green, raw | = 190g |
| 1 cup, mature seeds, green boiled | = 198g |
| 1 cup, mature seeds, sprouted, raw | = 80g |
| 1 cup, mature seeds, pink, raw | = 186g |
| 1 cup, mature seeds, pink, boiled | = 196g |

## NUTS

| | |
|---|---|
| 1 cup, *almond*, whole kernel, with skin, raw | = 152g |
| 1 cup, *almond*, whole kernel, skinned, raw | = 145g |
| 1 cup, *almond*, sticks, skinned, raw | = 133g |
| 1 cup, *almond*, slivered, skinned, raw | = 94g |
| 1 cup, *almond*, chopped, skinned, raw | = 129g |
| 1 cup, *almond*, ground, raw | = 102g |
| 1 cup, *almond*, paste, firmly packed | = 227g |
| 1 piece *almond*, whole kernel, raw | = 1g |
| | |
| 1 cup, *almond*, whole kernel, skinned, dry roasted, unsalted | = 142g |
| 1 cup, *almond*, whole kernel, skinned, dry roasted, salted | = 138g |
| 1 cup, *almond*, slivered, skinned, dry roasted, unsalted | = 115g |

# LEGUMES, NUTS, SEEDS and PRODUCTS

**Figure 49.** *Oil-roasted and salted cashew nuts*

# LEGUMES, NUTS, SEEDS and PRODUCTS

## NUTS

1 cup, *almond*, whole kernel, skinned, oil roasted, unsalted = 157g
1 cup, *almond*, whole kernel, skinned, oil roasted, salted   = 157g
1 cup, *almond* butter   = 256g

1 cup, *brazil*, whole kernel, with skin, raw   = 133g
1 piece *brazil*, whole kernel, with skin, raw   =   5g

1 cup, *cashew*, halves and whole, skinned, raw   = 125g
1 cup, *cashew*, chopped, skinned, raw   = 148g
1 cup, *cashew*, halves and whole, skinned, dry-roasted,   = 137g
1 cup, *cashew*, halves and whole, skinned, oil-roasted   = 130g
1 cup, *cashew* butter   = 256g

## NUTS

1 cup, *hazel*, whole, with skin, raw   = 138g
1 cup, *hazel*, ground, raw, firmly packed   = 145g
1 cup, *hazel*, ground, raw, loosely packed   = 112g
1 cup, *hazel*, whole, skinned, dry-roasted   = 129g

1 cup, *macadamia*, whole, skinned, raw   = 139g
1 cup, *macadamia*, skinned, dry-roasted   = 130g
1 cup, *macadamia*, skinned, oil-roasted   = 136g

1 cup, *pecan*, whole, with skin, raw   = 107g
1 cup, *pecan*, halves, with skin, raw   = 112g
1 cup, *pecan*, with skin, chopped, raw   = 110g
1 cup, *pecan*, halves, dry-roasted   = 101g

1 cup, *pili*, whole, with skin, raw   = 118g
1 cup, *pili*, halves and whole, skinned, fried, sweetened   = 157g
1 cup, *pili*, chopped, fried, sweetened   = 165g

# LEGUMES, NUTS, SEEDS and PRODUCTS

## NUTS

| | |
|---|---|
| 1 cup, *pine nuts*, skinned, raw | = 132g |
| 1 cup, *pine nuts*, skinned, dry-roasted | = 124g |
| | |
| 1 cup, *walnut*, chopped, raw | = 120g |
| 1 cup, *walnut*, ground, raw | = 92g |

## PEAS

| | |
|---|---|
| 1 cup, *chickpea*, mature seeds, raw | = 200g |
| 1 cup, *chickpea*, immature seeds, boiled | = 160g |
| 1 cup, *chickpea*, mature seeds, canned | = 250g |
| 1 cup, *chickpea* flour, stirred, spooned | = 90g |
| 1 cup, *chickpea*, hummus | = 245g |
| | |
| 1 cup, *cow pea*, mature seeds, raw | = 167g |
| 1 cup, *cow pea*, mature seeds, boiled | = 171g |
| | |
| 1 cup, *green pea*, mature seeds, whole, raw | = 150g |
| 1 cup, *green pea*, mature seeds, whole, boiled | = 175g |
| 1 cup, *green pea*, mature seeds, split, raw | = 200g |
| 1 cup, *green pea*, canned in water pack, drained | = 177g |
| 1 cup, *green pea*, mature seeds, whole, oil-roasted, with salt | = 123g |
| | |
| 1 cup, *peanut*, freshly harvested, with shell, raw | = 87g |
| 1 cup, *peanut*, freshly harvested, with shell, boiled | = 150g |
| 1 cup, *peanut*, dried with shell, boiled | = 73g |
| | |
| 1 cup, *peanut*, shelled, with skin, small nuts, raw | = 160g |
| 1 cup, *peanut*, shelled, with skin, large nuts, raw | = 156g |
| 1 cup, *peanut*, skinned, small nuts, raw | = 149g |
| 1 cup, *peanut*, skinned, large nuts, raw | = 140g |
| 1 cup, *peanut*, skinned, chopped, raw | = 132g |

# LEGUMES, NUTS, SEEDS and PRODUCTS

## PEAS

| | |
|---|---|
| 1 cup, *peanut*, skinned, oil-roasted, with salt | = 150g |
| 1 cup, *peanut*, skinned, dry-roasted with salt | = 142g |
| 1 cup, *peanut*, with skin-on, dry roasted, no salt | = 147g |
| 1 cup, *peanut*, flour, stirred, spooned | =  55g |
| 1 cup, *peanut butter*, smooth style | = 290g |
| 1 cup, *peanut butter*, with chunk style | = 260g |
| | |
| 1 cup, *pigeon pea*, mature seeds, raw | = 200g |
| 1 cup, *pigeon pea*, mature seeds, boiled | = 170g |
| 1 cup, *pigeon pea*, immature seeds, raw | = 150g |
| 1 cup, *pigeon pea*, immature, seeds, boiled | = 155g |

## SEEDS

| | |
|---|---|
| 1 cup, *poppy*, dried, raw | = 151g |
| 1 cup, *sesame*, dried, raw | = 128g |
| 1 cup, *squash*, dry-roasted, hulled | = 134g |
| 1 cup, *sunflower*, dry-roasted | = 126g |
| 1 cup, *watermelon*, dry-roasted, hulled | = 120g |

# DAIRY, EGG and PRODUCTS

# DAIRY and EGG PRODUCTS

**BUTTER**

| | |
|---|---|
| 1 stick, salted | = 113g |
| 1 cup, salted | = 227g |

**CHEESE**

| | |
|---|---|
| 1 cup, *blue,* crumbled, loosely pack | = 135g |
| 1 cup, *brick*, grated | = 113g |
| 1 cup, *brick*, diced | = 132g |
| 1 cup, *brie*, sliced | = 144g |
| 1 cup, *brie*, melted | = 240g |
| 1 cup, *camembert* | = 246g |
| | |
| 1 cup, *cheddar*, grated, fine | =  96g |
| 1 cup, *cheddar*, grated, coarse | = 113g |
| 1 cup, *cheddar*, diced | = 132g |
| 1 cup, *cheddar*, melted | = 244g |
| 1 cup, *cottage*, with small curd, loosely packed | = 225g |
| 1 cup, *cottage*, with large curd, firmly packed | = 210g |
| | |
| 1 cup, *cream* | = 230g |
| 1 cup, *feta*, crumbled | = 150g |
| 1 cup, *fontina* | = 108g |
| 1 cup, *limburger* | = 134g |
| 1 cup, *mozzarella*, grated | = 112g |
| | |
| 1 cup, *parmesan*, grated | =  80g |
| 1 cup, *ricotta* | = 124g |
| 1 cup, *swiss*, melted | = 244g |
| 1 cup, *pasteurized*, diced | = 140g |

# DAIRY, EGG and PRODUCTS

## CREAM

| | |
|---|---|
| 1 cup, fluid, half and half | = 242g |
| 1 cup, fluid, table cream | = 240g |
| 1 cup, light, whipping | = 239g |
| 1 cup, heavy, whipping | = 238g |
| 1 cup, sour | = 230g |

## MILK

| | |
|---|---|
| 1 cup, *fluid, whole* | = 245g |
| 1 cup, *fluid, low fat* | = 245g |
| 1 cup, *fluid, non fat* | = 245g |
| 1 cup, *dry, whole* | = 128g |
| 1 cup, *dry, non fat* | = 120g |
| 1 cup, *dry, buttermilk* | = 120g |
| 1 cup, *condensed, canned* | = 305g |
| 1 cup, *evaporated, canned* | = 252g |

## YOGURT

| | |
|---|---|
| 1 cup, *plain, whole milk* | = 245g |
| 1 cup, *plain, low fat* | = 245g |
| 1 cup, *plain, skim milk* | = 245g |

# DAIRY, EGG and PRODUCTS

## EGG

| | |
|---|---|
| 1 small, *chicken*, whole, raw | = 38g |
| 1 medium, *chicken*, whole, raw | = 44g |
| 1 large, *chicken*, whole, raw | = 50g |
| 1 extra-large, *chicken*, whole raw | = 56g |
| 1 jumbo, *chicken*, whole, raw | = 63g |
| | |
| 1 cup, *chicken*, whole, raw | = 243g |
| 1 cup, *chicken*, egg white, raw | = 243g |
| 1 large, *chicken*, egg white, raw | = 33g |
| 1 cup, *chicken*, egg yolk, raw | = 243g |
| 1 large, *chicken*, egg yolk, raw | = 17g |
| | |
| 1 large, *chicken*, whole, fried | = 46g |
| 1 large, *chicken*, whole, hard-boiled | = 50g |
| 1 cup, *chicken*, hard-boiled, chopped | = 136g |
| 1 cup, *chicken*, whole, dried | = 85g |
| 1 cup, *chicken*, egg yolk, dried | = 67g |
| 1 cup, *chicken*, egg white, dried | = 107g |
| | |
| 1 piece, *duck,* whole, fresh | = 70g |
| 1 piece, *goose*, whole, fresh | = 144g |
| 1 piece, *quail*, whole, fresh | = 9g |
| 1 piece, *turkey*, whole, fresh | = 79g |

# FISH, SHELLFISH and PRODUCTS

# FISH, SHELLFISH and PRODUCTS

**FISH**

| | |
|---|---|
| 1 piece fillet, *bass, striped*, raw | = 159g |
| 1 piece fillet, *bass, striped*, cooked in oven | = 124g |
| 1 piece fillet, *bluefish*, raw | = 150g |
| 1 piece fillet, *bluefish*, cooked in oven | = 117g |
| 1 piece fillet, *burbot*, raw | = 116g |
| 1 piece fillet, *burbot*, cooked in oven | = 90g |
| | |
| 1 piece fillet, *butterfish*, raw | = 32g |
| 1 piece fillet, *butterfish*, cooked in oven | = 25g |
| 1 piece fillet, *carp*, raw | = 218g |
| 1 piece fillet, *carp*, cooked in oven | = 170g |
| 1 piece fillet, *cisco*, raw | = 79g |
| | |
| 1 piece fillet, *cod*, Atlantic, raw | = 231g |
| 1 piece fillet, *cod* Atlantic, cooked in oven | = 180g |
| 1 piece fillet, *cod*, Pacific, raw | = 116g |
| 1 piece fillet, *cod* Pacific, cooked in oven | = 90g |
| 1 piece fillet, *croaker*, raw | = 79g |
| | |
| 1 piece fillet, *cusk*, raw | = 122g |
| 1 piece fillet, *cusk*, cooked in oven | = 95g |
| 1 piece fillet, *flounder*, raw | = 163g |
| 1 piece fillet, *flounder*, cooked in oven | = 127g |
| 1 piece fillet, *grouper*, raw | = 259g |
| 1 piece fillet, *grouper*, cooked in oven | = 202g |
| | |
| 1 piece fillet, *haddock*, raw | = 193g |
| 1 piece fillet, *haddock*, cooked in oven | = 150g |
| 1 piece fillet, *halibut*, raw | = 408g |
| 1 piece fillet, *halibut*, cooked in oven | = 318g |

# FISH, SHELLFISH and PRODUCTS

## FISH

| | |
|---|---|
| 1 piece fillet, *herring*, raw | = 184g |
| 1 piece fillet, *herring*, cooked in oven | = 144g |
| 1 piece fillet, *lingcod*, raw | = 193g |
| 1 piece fillet, *lingcod*, cooked in oven | = 151g |
| 1 piece fillet, *mackerel*, raw | = 225g |
| 1 piece fillet, *mackerel*, cooked in oven | = 176g |
| | |
| 1 piece fillet, *mackerel, Spanish*, raw | = 187g |
| 1 piece fillet, *mackerel, Spanish*, cooked in oven | = 146g |
| 1 piece fillet, *milkfish*, raw | = 116g |
| 1 piece fillet, *milkfish*, cooked in oven | = 87g |
| | |
| 1 piece fillet, *mullet, striped*, raw | = 119g |
| 1 piece fillet, *mullet, striped*, cooked in oven | = 93g |
| 1 piece fillet, *perch*, raw | = 60g |
| 1 piece fillet, *perch*, cooked in oven | = 46g |
| | |
| 1 piece fillet, *pout*, raw | = 352g |
| 1 piece fillet, *pout*, cooked in oven | = 274g |
| 1 piece fillet, *pike*, raw | = 198g |
| 1 piece fillet, *pike*, cooked in oven | = 124g |
| 1 piece fillet, *pollock*, raw | = 386g |
| 1 piece fillet, *pollock*, cooked in oven | = 302g |
| | |
| 1 piece fillet, *pompano*, raw | = 112g |
| 1 piece fillet, *pompano*, cooked in oven | = 88g |
| 1 piece fillet, *rockfish*, raw | = 191g |
| 1 piece filet, *rockfish*, cooked in oven | = 149g |
| 1 piece fillet, *sablefish*, raw | = 386g |
| 1 piece fillet, *sablefish*, cooked in oven | = 302g |

# FISH, SHELLFISH and PRODUCTS

**FISH**

| | |
|---|---|
| 1 piece fillet, *salmon*, Atlanta, raw | = 396g |
| 1 piece fillet, *salmon*, Atlanta, cooked in oven | = 308g |
| 1 piece fillet, *salmon*, pink, raw | = 318g |
| 1 piece fillet, *salmon, pink*, cooked in oven | = 248g |
| | |
| 1 piece fillet, *scup*, raw | = 64g |
| 1 piece fillet, *scup*, cooked in oven | = 50g |
| 1 piece fillet, *sea bass*, raw | = 129g |
| 1 piece fillet, *sea bass*, cooked in oven | = 101g |
| | |
| 1 piece fillet, *sea trout*, raw | = 238g |
| 1 piece fillet, *sea trout*, cooked in oven | = 186g |
| 1 piece fillet, *shad*, raw | = 184g |
| 1 piece fillet, *shad*, cooked in oven | = 144g |
| 1 piece fillet, *sheepshead*, raw | = 238g |
| 1 piece fillet, *sheepshead*, cooked in oven | = 186g |
| | |
| 1 piece fillet, *snapper*, raw | = 218g |
| 1 piece fillet, *snapper*, cooked in oven | = 170g |
| 1 piece fillet, *spot*, raw | = 64g |
| 1 piece fillet, *spot*, cooked in oven | = 50g |
| 1 piece fillet, *tilapia*, raw | = 116g |
| 1 piece fillet, *tilapia*, cooked in oven | = 87g |
| | |
| 1 piece fillet, *tilefish*, raw | = 386g |
| 1 piece fillet, *tilefish*, cooked in oven | = 300g |
| 1 piece fillet, *trout*, raw | = 79g |
| 1 piece fillet, *trout*, cooked in oven | = 62g |
| 1 piece fillet, *turbot*, raw | = 408g |
| 1 piece fillet, *turbot*, cooked in oven | = 318g |

# FISH, SHELLFISH and PRODUCTS

Figure 50. *A fillet of pink salmon*

# FISH, SHELLFISH and PRODUCTS

### FISH

| | |
|---|---|
| 1 piece fillet, *whitefish*, raw | = 198g |
| 1 piece fillet, *whitefish*, cooked in oven | = 154g |
| 1 piece fillet, *whiting*, raw | = 92g |
| 1 piece fillet, *whiting*, cooked in oven | = 72g |

### SHELLFISH

| | |
|---|---|
| 1 piece leg, *crab, King*, raw | = 172g |
| 1 piece leg, *crab, King* steamed | = 134g |
| 1 piece, *crab, blue*, raw | = 21g |
| 1 cup, *crab, blue*, steamed, flaked | = 118g |
| 1 piece, *crab, Dungeness*, raw | = 163g |
| 1 piece, *crab, Dungeness*, steamed | = 127g |
| 1 piece *lobster*, raw | = 150g |
| 1 cup, *lobster*, steamed, flaked | = 145g |
| 1 cup, *clams*, with shell, raw | = 227g |
| 1 cup, *mussels*, with shell, raw | = 150g |
| 1 cup, *oyster*, shelled, raw | = 248g |

### FISH and SHELLFISH PRODUCTS

| | |
|---|---|
| 1 stick, fish, 4 inches x 2 inches x ½ inch | = 57g |
| 1 cup, sardines in tomato sauce, drained | = 89g |
| 1 cup, tuna, canned in oil, chunks, drained | = 146g |
| 1 cup, tuna, canned in water, chunks, drained | = 154g |
| 1 cup, fish tofu, cubed 3/4-inch, uncooked | = 144g |
| 1 cup, fish tofu, cubed 3/4-inch, boiled | = 148g |
| 1 cup, squid balls, uncooked | = 162g |
| 1 cup, squid balls, boiled | = 168g |
| 1 cup, salmon ball, uncooked | = 248g |
| 1 cup, salmon ball, boiled | = 258g |
| 1 cup, crab stick, cut into 1 ½ inches long, uncooked | = 148g |
| 1 cup, crab stick, cut into 1 ½ inches long, boiled | = 162g |

# MEAT, POULTRY and PRODUCTS

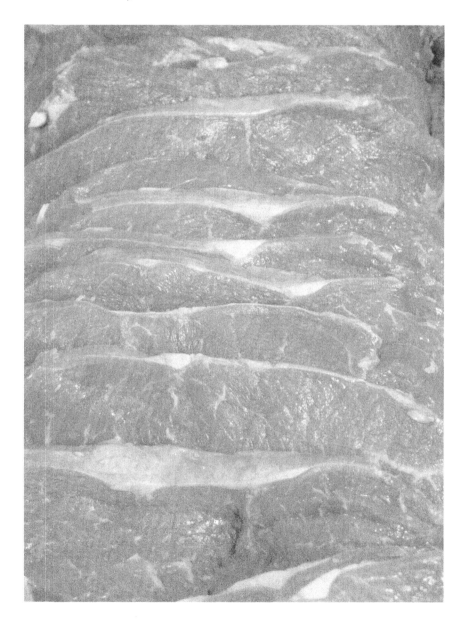

# MEAT, POULTRY and PRODUCTS

**BEEF**

| | |
|---|---|
| 1 steak, *short loin, t-bone*, lean only, grilled | = 360g |
| 1 steak, *tenderloin*, with lean and fat, grilled | = 117g |
| 1 steak, *toploin*, with lean and fat, grilled | = 119g |
| 1 steak, *top sirloin*, with lean and fat, grilled | = 384g |
| | |
| 1 steak, *short loin, porter house*, lean only, grilled | = 421g |
| 1 steak, *short loin, t-bone steak*, grilled | = 363g |
| 1 steak, *top round*, lean only, grilled | = 277g |
| 1 steak, *top shoulder blade*, grilled | = 186g |
| | |
| 1 cup, *sirloin*, large dice, raw | = 235g |
| 1 cup, *sirloin*, ground, raw | = 238g |

**PORK**

| | |
|---|---|
| 1 chop, *loin*, with lean and fat, raw | = 117g |
| 1 chop, *loin*, with lean and fat, braised | = 89g |
| 1 chop, *loin*, with lean and fat, broiled | = 87g |
| 1 chop, *loin*, with lean and fat, roasted | = 89g |
| | |
| 1 chop, *loin*, lean only, raw | = 106g |
| 1 chop, *loin*, lean only, braised | = 80g |
| 1 chop, *loin*, lean only, broiled | = 79g |
| 1 chop, *loin*, lean only, roasted | = 81g |
| | |
| 1 chop, *loin blade*, bone-in, raw | = 263g |
| 1 chop, *loin blade*, bone-in, braised | = 206g |
| 1 chop, *loin blade*, bone-in, broiled | = 219g |
| | |
| 1 chop, *center loin*, lean and fat, raw | = 199g |
| 1 chop, *center loin*, lean and fat, braised | = 187g |
| 1 chop, *center loin*, lean and fat, broiled | = 157g |

# MEAT, POULTRY and PRODUCTS

## PORK

| | |
|---|---|
| 1 chop, *center loin*, lean only, raw | = 178g |
| 1 chop, *center loin*, lean only, braised | = 187g |
| 1 chop, *center loin*, lean only, broiled | = 146g |
| 1 cup, *center loin*, lean only, ground, raw | = 228g |
| | |
| 1 chop, *sirloin*, lean and fat, braised | = 180g |
| 1 chop, *sirloin*, lean and fat, broiled | = 195g |
| 1 chop, *top loin*, lean and fat, raw | = 185g |
| 1 chop, *top loin*, lean and fat, braised | = 135g |
| 1 chop, *top loin*, lean and fat, broiled | = 145g |
| | |
| 1 cup, *heart*, braised | = 145g |
| 1 cup, *kidney*, braised | = 140g |

## PORK PRODUCTS

| | |
|---|---|
| 1 cup, chorizo de bilbao, canned, sliced | = 130g |
| 1 cup, chorizo de bilbao, canned, diced | = 175g |
| 1 cup, bacon diced, uncooked | = 132g |
| 1 cup, bacon, diced, pan-fried | = 150g |
| 1 cup, sausage Vienna, canned, minced, firmly packed | = 187g |
| 1 cup sausage Vienna, canned, minced, loosely packed | = 143g |
| 1 cup, pork crackling, coarsely chopped | = 17g |
| 1 cup, pork cracklings, finely chopped, firmly packed | = 63g |
| 1 cup, pork cracklings, loosely chopped, loosely packed | = 43g |
| 1 cup, pork cured meat (tocino), with lean and fat, uncooked | = 270g |
| 1 cup, pork cured meat (tocino), with lean and fat, fried | = 179g |
| 1 cup, pork ham cured meat, roasted | = 140g |

# MEAT, POULTRY and PRODUCTS

## POULTRY

| | |
|---|---|
| 1 piece *breast*, skinless, bone less, raw | = 272g |
| 1 piece *drumstick*, with skin, raw | = 133g |
| 1 piece *thigh*, with skin, raw | = 193g |
| 1 piece *wing*, with skin, raw | = 107g |
| 1 piece *heart*, raw | = 6g |
| 1 piece *liver*, raw | = 44g |
| 1 cup, *breast*, skinless, dice, raw | = 245g |
| 1 cup, *breast*, skinless, ground, raw | = 236g |
| | |
| 1 cup, *breast*, skinless, diced, boiled, firmly packed | = 163g |
| 1 cup, *breast*, skinless, diced, boiled, loosely packed | = 136g |
| 1 cup, *breast*, skinless, ground, boiled, firmly packed | = 216g |
| 1 cup, *breast*, skinless, ground, boiled, loosely packed | = 123g |
| 1 cup, *breast*, skinless, diced, roasted, firmly packed | = 167g |
| 1 cup, *breast*, skinless, diced, roasted, loosely packed | = 137g |
| | |
| 1 piece *quail* meat, raw | = 92g |
| 1 piece *quail* breast, raw | = 56g |
| 1 piece *squab* meat with skin, raw | = 199g |
| 1 piece *squab* meat, no skin, raw | = 168g |
| | |
| 1 piece *turkey* gizzard, raw | = 63g |
| 1 piece *turkey* heart, raw | = 24g |
| 1 piece, *turkey* liver, raw | = 78g |

## POULTRY PRODUCTS

| | |
|---|---|
| 1 cup, chicken cured meat (tocino), uncooked | = 245g |
| 1 cup, chicken cured meat (tocino), fried | = 165g |
| 1 piece, chicken nugget, pre-cooked | = 18g |
| 1 piece, chicken strip, pre-cooked | = 36g |

# FATS and OILS

# FATS and OILS

### LARD
| | |
|---|---|
| 1 cup, firmly packed | = 205g |

### MAYONNAISE
| | |
|---|---|
| 1 cup, regular and light | = 250g |
| 1 cup, fat-free | = 255g |

### MARGARINE
| | |
|---|---|
| 1 stick, regular, soybean, hydrogenated | = 113g |
| 1 cup, regular, soybean, hydrogenated | = 227g |
| 1 cup, vegetable oil spread | = 233g |

### OIL
| | |
|---|---|
| 1 cup, *almond* | = 218g |
| 1 cup, *avocado* | = 218g |
| 1 cup, *canola* | = 218g |
| 1 cup, *coconut* | = 216g |
| 1 cup, *cod liver* | = 218g |
| 1 cup, *corn* | = 219g |
| 1 cup, *grape seed* | = 218g |
| 1 cup, *hazelnut* | = 218g |
| 1 cup, *mustard* | = 218g |
| 1 cup, *olive* | = 218g |
| 1 cup, *palm* | = 216g |
| 1 cup, *peanut* | = 218g |
| 1 cup, *poppy seed* | = 218g |
| 1 cup, *safflower* | = 216g |
| 1 cup, *sesame* | = 218g |
| 1 cup, *soya* | = 216g |
| 1 cup, *vegetable* | = 217g |
| 1 cup, *walnut* | = 218g |

# FATS and OILS

## SALAD DRESSING

| | |
|---|---|
| 1 cup, *caesar*, regular | = 235g |
| 1 cup, *caesar*, reduced fat | = 245g |
| 1 cup, *caesar,* fat-free | = 272g |
| 1 cup, *cheese*, regular | = 245g |
| 1 cup, *cheese*, fat-free | = 265g |
| | |
| 1 cup, *coleslaw*, regular | = 250g |
| 1 cup, *coleslaw*, reduced fat | = 269g |
| 1 cup, *french*, regular | = 260g |
| 1 cup, *french*, reduced fat | = 260g |
| 1 cup, *french*, reduced fat | = 255g |
| | |
| 1 cup, *honey* mustard, regular | = 240g |
| 1 cup, *honey* mustard, fat-free | = 240g |
| 1 cup, *italian*, regular | = 230g |
| 1 cup, *italian*, reduced fat | = 216g |
| 1 cup, *italian*, fat-free | = 230g |
| | |
| 1 cup, *peppercorn*, regular | = 214g |
| 1 cup, *poppyseed*, regular | = 264g |
| 1 cup, *ranch*, regular | = 240g |
| 1 cup, *ranch*, fat-free | = 224g |
| 1 cup, *russian*, regular | = 245g |
| 1 cup, *russian*, reduced fat | = 260g |
| | |
| 1 cup, *thousand island*, regular | = 250g |
| 1 cup, *thousand island*, reduced fat | = 245g |
| 1 cup, *thousand island,* fat-free | = 255g |
| 1 cup, *sesame seed*, regular | = 245g |

# FATS and OILS

## SALAD DRESSING

| | |
|---|---|
| 1 cup, *sour cream*, cultured, regular | = 235g |
| 1 cup, *sour cream*, cultured, reduced fat | = 230g |
| 1 cup, *sour cream*, cultured, fat-free | = 230g |
| 1 cup, *sweet and sour*, regular | = 250g |
| 1 cup, *vinegar and oil*, regular | = 250g |

## SHORTENING

| | |
|---|---|
| 1 cup, *palm* | = 205g |
| 1 cup, *soybean* | = 205g |
| 1 cup, *vegetable oil* | = 205g |

# SEASONINGS and CONDIMENTS

# SEASONINGS and CONDIMENTS

## SEASONINGS

| | |
|---|---|
| 1 cup, *banana artificial flavoring* | = 226g |
| 1 cup, *lemon artificial flavoring* | = 225g |
| 1 cup, *vanilla artificial flavoring* | = 231g |
| 1 cup, *caregeenan powder* | = 178g |
| 1 cup, *curing salt*, firmly packed | = 286g |
| 1 cup, *curing salt*, loosely packed | = 255g |
| | |
| 1 cup, *ham spice*, firmly packed | = 211g |
| 1 cup, *ham spice*, loosely packed | = 166g |
| 1 cup *isolate powder* | = 104g |
| 1 cup, *monosodium glutamate* | = 201g |
| | |
| 1 cup paste, *mudfish*, uncooked | = 246g |
| 1 cup paste, *shrimp fry*, raw, pressed | = 251g |
| 1 cup paste, *shrimp fry*, sautéed, firmly packed | = 259g |
| 1 cup, *phosphate powder*, firmly packed | = 136g |
| 1 cup, *phosphate powder*, loosely packed | = 158g |
| | |
| 1 cup, *salt*, coarse | = 122g |
| 1 cup, *salt*, free-running | = 285g |
| 1 cup, seasoning, *aromat powder* | = 172g |
| 1 cup, seasoning, *chicken powder*, firmly packed | = 269g |
| 1 cup. Seasoning, *chicken powder*, loosely packed | = 197g |
| | |
| 1 cup, vinegar, *apple cider* | = 235g |
| 1 cup, vinegar, *balsamic* | = 265g |
| 1 cup, vinegar, *red wine* | = 250g |
| 1 cup, vinegar, *rice* | = 230g |
| 1 cup, vinegar, *white wine* | = 239g |
| 1 cup, vinegar, *sugar cane* | = 240g |

# SEASONINGS and CONDIMENTS

## SEASONINGS

| | |
|---|---|
| 1 cup, *Vitamin C powder* | = 202g |
| 1 cup, *Wasabi powder* | = 100g |

## CONDIMENTS

| | |
|---|---|
| 1 cup, castup, *banana* | = 275g |
| 1 cup, catsup, *tomato* | = 275g |
| | |
| 1 cup, gravy, *au jus* | = 240g |
| 1 cup, gravy, *chicken* | = 233g |
| 1 cup, gravy, *mushroom* | = 238g |
| 1 cup, gravy, *turkey* | = 238g |
| | |
| 1 cup, sauce, *barbeque* | = 275g |
| 1 cup, sauce, *cheese* | = 250g |
| 1 cup, sauce, *chili-tomato* | = 280g |
| 1 cup, sauce, *duck* | = 270g |
| | |
| 1 cup, sauce, *fish, clear* | = 285g |
| 1 cup, sauce, *fish, dark* | = 301g |
| 1 cup, sauce, *hoisin* | = 320g |
| 1 cup, sauce, *lechon* | = 275g |
| | |
| 1 cup, sauce, *mustard* | = 280g |
| 1 cup, sauce, *oyster* | = 290g |
| 1 cup, sauce, *pizza* | = 260g |
| 1 cup, sauce, *plum* | = 310g |
| | |
| 1 cup, sauce, *salsa* | = 260g |
| 1 cup, sauce, *dark* | = 275g |
| 1 cup, sauce, *light* | = 275g |

# SEASONINGS and CONDIMENTS

## CONDIMENTS

| | |
|---|---|
| 1 cup, sauce, *spaghetti* | = 250g |
| 1 cup, sauce, *stir-fry vegetarian* | = 308g |
| 1 cup, sauce, *sweet and sour* | = 290g |
| 1 cup, sauce, *tartar* | = 256g |
| | |
| 1 cup, sauce, *teriyaki* | = 290g |
| 1 cup, sauce, *tonkatsu* | = 262g |
| 1 cup, sauce, *tomato* | = 256g |
| 1 cup, sauce, *white* | = 248g |
| 1 cup, sauce, *Worcestershire* | = 265g |
| | |
| 1 cup, vinaigrette | = 188g |

# BAKING INGREDIENTS

# SELECTED BAKING INGREDIENTS

| | |
|---|---|
| 1 cup, *baking powder* | = 220g |
| 1 cup, *baking soda* | = 218g |
| 1 cup, *cake sprinkles* multi-colored | = 186g |
| 1 cup, *caramel crunch* | =  65g |
| | |
| 1 cup, *chocolate bar*, grated | = 130g |
| 1 cup, *chocolate lentils, bud type* | = 196g |
| 1 cup, *chocolate lentils* | = 207g |
| 1 cup, *chocolate droplets*, semi-sweet | = 160g |
| | |
| 1 cup, *chocolate candies*, egg-shaped | = 306g |
| 1 cup, *chocolate fudge* | = 300g |
| 1 cup, *chocolate spread* | = 300g |
| 1 cup, *chocolate syrup* | = 280g |
| | |
| 1 cup, *cocoa powder*, unsweetened, sifted | =  90g |
| 1 cup, *cocoa powder*, unsweetened, unsifted | = 100g |
| 1 cup, *cream of tartar* | = 148g |
| 1 cup, *gelatin*, granulated, unflavored, firmly packed | = 165g |
| 1 cup, *gelatin*, granulated, unflavored, loosely packed | = 155g |
| | |
| 1 cup, *glucose* | = 340g |
| 1 cup, *gulaman bar*, shredded, uncooked | =  10g |
| 1 cup, *honey* | = 331g |
| 1 cup, *marsmallow*, regular | =  50g |
| 1 cup, *marsmallow*, mini size | =  54g |
| 1 cup, *molasses* | = 352g |
| | |
| 1 cup, *sugar, brown*, firmly packed | = 220g |
| 1 cup, *sugar, brown*, loosely packed | = 140g |
| 1 cup, *sugar, dark brown*, firmly packed | = 244g |
| 1 cup, *sugar, dark brown*, loosely packed | = 175g |

# SELECTED BAKING INGREDIENTS

**Figure 51.** *Chocolate candies*

# SELECTED BAKING INGREDIENTS

1 cup, *sugar, soft brown*, firmly packed      = 168g

1 cup, *sugar, soft brown*, loosely packed      = 120g

1 cup, *sugar, caster*      = 206g

1 cup, *sugar, muscovado*, firmly packed      = 237g

1 cup, *sugar, muscuvado*, loosely packed      = 157g

1 cup, *sugar, powdered*, sifted, spooned      = 100g

1 cup, *sugar, powdered*, unsifted, spooned      = 120g

1 cup, *sugar, washed*      = 220g

1 cup, *sugar, granulated*      = 200g

1 cup, syrup, *agave*      = 220g

1 cup, syrup, *corn, dark*      = 332g

1 cup, syrup, *high-fructose*      = 300g

1 cup, syrup, *grenadine*      = 320g

1 cup, syrup, *light*      = 341g

1 cup, syrup, *malt*      = 390g

1 cup, syrup, *maple*      = 312g

1 cup, syrup, *pancake*      = 320g

1 cup syrup, *sorghum*      = 330g

1 cup, topping, *caramel*      = 328g

1 cup, topping, *jam*      = 320g

1 cup, topping, *jellies*      = 336g

1 cup, topping, *marmalade*      = 320g

# DRINKS

# DRINKS

## ALCOHOLIC DRINKS

| | |
|---|---|
| 1 fluid ounce, *beer, regular* | = 29.7g |
| 1 fluid ounce, *beer, light* | = 29.5g |
| 1 fluid ounce, *daiquiri cocktail* | = 30.5g |
| 1 fluid ounce, *piña colada cocktail* | = 32.6g |
| 1 fluid ounce, *tequila sunrise cocktail* | = 31.1g |
| | |
| 1 fluid ounce, liquor, *gin 90 proof* | = 27.8g |
| 1 fluid ounce, liquor, *rum 80 proof* | = 27.8g |
| 1 fluid ounce, liquor, *whiskey 86 proof* | = 27.8g |
| 1 fluid ounce, liquor, *vodka 80 proof* | = 27.8g |
| 1 fluid ounce, liqueur, *crème de menthe 72 proof* | = 33.6g |
| 1 fluid ounce, liqueur, *coffee 53 proof* | = 34.8g |
| 1 fluid ounce, liqueur, *coffee-cream 34 proof* | = 31.1g |
| | |
| 1 fluid ounce, wine, red, *Barbera* | = 29.4g |
| 1 fluid ounce, wine, red, *Burgundy* | = 29.5g |
| 1 fluid ounce, wine, red, *Cabernet Franc* | = 29.0g |
| 1 fluid ounce, wine, red, *Cabernet Sauvignon* | = 29.0g |
| 1 fluid ounce, wine, red, *Carigname* | = 29.4g |
| | |
| 1 fluid ounce, wine, red, *Claret* | = 29.4g |
| 1 fluid ounce, wine, red, *Gamay* | = 29.4g |
| 1 fluid ounce, wine, red, *Lemberger* | = 29.4g |
| 1 fluid ounce, wine, red, *Merlot* | = 29.4g |
| 1 fluid ounce, wine, red, *Mouvedre* | = 29.4g |
| | |
| 1 fluid ounce, wine, red, *Pinot Noir* | = 29.4g |
| 1 fluid ounce, wine, red *Petite Sirah* | = 29.5g |
| 1 fluid ounce, wine, red, *Sangiovese* | = 29.4g |
| 1 fluid ounce, wine, red, *Syrah* | = 29.5g |
| 1 fluid ounce, wine, red, *Zinfandel* | = 29.4g |

# DRINKS

## ALCOHOLIC DRINKS

| | |
|---|---|
| 1 fluid ounce, wine, white, *Chardonnay* | = 29.3g |
| 1 fluid ounce, wine, white, *Chenin Blanc* | = 29.5g |
| 1 fluid ounce, wine, white, *Gewurztraminer* | = 29.5g |
| 1 fluid ounce, wine, white, *Muscat* | = 30.0g |
| 1 fluid ounce, wine, white, *Muller Thurgau* | = 29.5g |
| 1 fluid ounce, wine, white, *Pinot Blanc* | = 29.3g |
| 1 fluid ounce, wine, white, *Pinot Gris* | = 29.3g |
| 1 fluid ounce, wine, white, *Riesling* | = 29.6g |
| 1 fluid ounce, wine, white, *Semillon* | = 29.5g |
| 1 fluid ounce, wine, white, *Sauvignon Blanc* | = 29.3g |
| 1 fluid ounce, wine, cooking | = 29.0g |
| 1 fluid ounce, wine, dessert | = 29.5g |
| 1 fluid ounce, wine, sake | = 29.1g |

## CARBONATED DRINKS

| | |
|---|---|
| 1 fluid ounce, *club soda* | = 29.6g |
| 1 fluid ounce, *cola, regular* | = 30.7g |
| 1 fluid ounce, *cola, light* | = 29.6g |
| 1 fluid ounce, *cream soda* | = 30.9g |
| 1 fluid ounce, *ginger ale* | = 31.0g |
| 1 fluid ounce, *grape soda* | = 31.0g |
| 1 fluid ounce, *lemon-lime soda* | = 30.8g |
| 1 fluid ounce, *root beer* | = 30.8g |
| 1 fluid ounce, *sprite* | = 30.8g |
| 1 fluid ounce, *tonic water* | = 30.5g |

# DRINKS

### ENERGY DRINKS

| | |
|---|---|
| 1 fluid ounce, *Ensure Nutritional Shake* | = 31.8g |
| 1 fluid ounce, *Ensure Plus* | = 31.5g |
| 1 fluid ounce, *Powerade* | = 30.5g |
| 1 fluid ounce, *Red Bull* | =  8.4g |

### JUICE DRINKS

| | |
|---|---|
| 1 fluid ounce, *acai berry* juice drink | = 30.8g |
| 1 fluid ounce, *cranberry-apple* juice drink | = 30.6g |
| 1 fluid ounce, *cranberry-apricot* juice drink | = 30.6g |
| 1 fluid ounce, *cranberry-grape* juice drink | = 30.6g |
| 1 fluid-ounce, *guava-passion* juice drink | = 30.3g |
| 1 fluid ounce, *grape juice* drink | = 31.3g |
| 1 fluid ounce, *orange juice* drink | = 31.0g |
| 1 fluid ounce, *orange-apricot* juice drink | = 31.2g |
| 1 fluid ounce, *peach-mango* juice drink | = 30.8g |
| 1 fluid ounce, *pineapple-grapefruit* juice drink | = 31.3g |
| 1 fluid ounce, *pineapple-orange* juice drink | = 31.3g |
| 1 fluid ounce, *strawberry-banana* juice drink | = 30.3g |
| 1 fluid ounce, *strawberry-kiwi juice* drink | = 30.3g |

### NON-ALCOHOLIC DRINKS

| | |
|---|---|
| 1 fluid ounce, *coffee*, brewed from grounds | = 29.6g |
| 1 fluid ounce, *tea*, black, brewed | = 29.6g |
| 1 fluid ounce, *tea*, chamomile, brewed | = 29.6g |
| 1 fluid ounce, *water,* bottled | = 29.6g |
| 1 fluid ounce, *water,* with added minerals | = 29.6g |
| 1 fluid ounce, *water*, tap | = 29.6g |

# EDIBLE PORTION of SELECTED INGREDIENTS

# EDIBLE PORTION of SELECTED INGREDIENTS

## CEREALS, TUBERS and VEGETABLES

| FOOD and SCIENTIFIC NAME | PERCENT EDIBLE PORTION |
|---|---|
| **Arrowroot** (*Maranta arundinacea*) | 85 |
| **Cassava tuber** (*Manihot esculenta*) | 79 |
| **Corn** (*Zea mays*) | 36 |
| **Potato** (*Solanum tuberosum*) | 75 |
| **Sweet potato tuber** (*Ipomoea batatas*) | 77 |
| **Sunchoke** (*Helianthus tuberosus*) | 69 |
| **Taro tuber** (*Colocasia esculenta*) | 82 |
| **Yam** (*Dioscorea spp.*) | 85 |
| **Yautia** (*Xanthosoma nigrum*) | 95 |
| **Amaranth leaves** (*Amaranth spp.*) | 94 |
| **Amaranth spineless leaves** (*Amaranthus gracilis*) | 72 |
| **Artichoke** (*Cynara scolymus*) | 40 |
| **Arugula** (*Eruca sativa*) | 60 |
| **Asparagus** (*Asparagus officinalis*) | 53 |
| **Bamboo shoot** (*Bambusa spinosa*) | 94 |
| **Banana blossom** (*Musa errans*) | 52 |

# EDIBLE PORTION of SELECTED INGREDIENTS

## CEREALS, TUBERS and VEGETABLES

| FOOD and SCIENTIFIC NAME | PERCENT EDIBLE PORTION |
|---|---|
| **Beets** (*Beta vulgaris*) | 75 |
| **Bitter gourd fruit** (*Momordica charantia*) | 83 |
| **Bitter gourd leaves** (*Momordica charantia*) | 42 |
| **Black nightshade** (*Solanum nigrum*) | 61 |
| **Broccoli** (*Brassica oleracea var. italica*) | 61 |
| **Cabbage bok choi** (*Brassica rapa chinensis grp.*) | 88 |
| **Cabbage, Chinese** (*Brassica rapa chinensis grp.*) | 95 |
| **Cabbage green** (*Brassica oleracea capitata grp.*) | 81 |
| **Cabbage red** (*Brassica oleracea capitata grp.*) | 83 |
| **Calabash** (*Lagenaria siceraria*) | 77 |
| **Carrot** (*Daucus carrota*) | 86 |
| **Cauliflower** (*Brassica oleracea botrytis grp.*) | 63 |
| **Celery** (*Apium graveolens*) | 89 |
| **Celery, Chinese** (*Apium graveolens*) | 76 |
| **Chayote fruit** (*Sechium edule*) | 85 |
| **Chayote leaves** (*Sechium edule*) | 35 |

# EDIBLE PORTION of SELECTED INGREDIENTS

## CEREALS, TUBERS and VEGETABLES

| FOOD and SCIENTIFIC NAME | PERCENT EDIBLE PORTION |
|---|---|
| **Coconut shoot** (*Cocus nucifera*) | 34 |
| **Collards** (*Brassica oleracea var. virides*) | 57 |
| **Cucumber** (*Cucumis sativus*) | 77 |
| **Endive** (*Cichorium endivia*) | 79 |
| **Cowpea pods** (*Vigna unguiculata*) | 89 |
| **Eggplant** (*Solanum melongena*) | 86 |
| **Fava bean pods** (*Vicia faba*) | 97 |
| **Fern** (*Athyrium esculentum*) | 59 |
| **Garden cress** (*Lepidium sativum*) | 71 |
| **Garlic** (Allium sativum) | 86 |
| **Ginger root** (Zingiber officinale) | 93 |
| **Horseradish pod** (*Moringa oleifera*) | 50 |
| **Horseradish leaves** (*Moringa oleifera*) | 59 |
| **Hyacinth bean pods** (*Dolichos lablab*) | 88 |
| **Jute leaves** (*Corchorus olitorius*) | 52 |
| **Kale** (*Brassica oleracea acephala grp.*) | 72 |

# EDIBLE PORTION of SELECTED INGREDIENTS

## CEREALS, TUBERS and VEGETABLES

| FOOD and SCIENTIFIC NAME | PERCENT EDIBLE PORTION |
|---|---|
| **Kohlrabi** (*Brassica gongylodes grp*) | 46 |
| **Lemon grass** (*Collinsonia canadensis*) | 65 |
| **Lettuce boston** (*Lactuca sativa var. capitata*) | 74 |
| **Lettuce icerberg** (*Lactuca sativa var. capitata*) | 95 |
| **Lettuce green leaf** (*Lactuca sativa var. crispa*) | 64 |
| **Lettuce red leaf** (*Lactuca sativa var. crispa*) | 80 |
| **Lettuce romaine** (*Lactuca sativa var. logifolia*) | 94 |
| **Lima bean pods** (*Phaseolus lunatus*) | 44 |
| **Malabar spinach** (*Basella alba*) | 67 |
| **Morning glory leaves** (*Ipomoea alba*) | 49 |
| **Mung bean sprout** (Phaseolus aureus) | 91 |
| **Mushroom champignon** (*Agaricus bisporus*) | 97 |
| **Mushroom chanterelle** (*Cantharelles cibarices*) | 100 |
| **Mushroom cloud ear** (*Auricularia polytricha*) | 99 |
| **Mushroom common split gill** (*Schizophyllum commune*) | 92 |
| **Mushroom enoki** (*Flammulina veleptripes*) | 84 |

# EDIBLE PORTION of SELECTED INGREDIENTS

## CEREALS, TUBERS and VEGETABLES

| FOOD and SCIENTIFIC NAME | PERCENT EDIBLE PORTION |
|---|---|
| **Mushroom oyster** (*Pleurotus ostreatus*) | 89 |
| **Mushroom portabella** (*Agaricus bisporus*) | 97 |
| **Mushroom shiitake** (*Lentinus edodes*) | 100 |
| **Mustard greens** (*Brassica juracea*) | 93 |
| **New Zealand Spinach** (*Tetragonia tetragonioides*) | 72 |
| **Okra** (*Abelmoschus esculentus*) | 88 |
| **Onion** (*Allium sepa*) | 90 |
| **Papaya fruit unripe** (*Carica papaya*) | 64 |
| **Parsley** (*Petroselinum crispum*) | 95 |
| **Pechay** (*Brassica rapa Pekinensis grp*) | 94 |
| **Pepper chili fruit** (*Capsicum frutescens*) | 96 |
| **Pepper chili leaves** (*Capsicum frutescens*) | 42 |
| **Pepper green finger fruit** (*Capsicum annum*) | 71 |
| **Pepper jalapeño** (*Capsicum annum*) | 92 |
| **Pepper sweet** (*Capsicum annum*) | 95 |
| **Pigeon pea pods** (*Cajanus cajan*) | 51 |

# EDIBLE PORTION of SELECTED INGREDIENTS

## CEREALS, TUBERS and VEGETABLES

| FOOD and SCIENTIFIC NAME | PERCENT EDIBLE PORTION |
|---|---|
| **Purslane** (*Portulaca oleracea*) | 61 |
| **Radicchio** (*Cichorium intybus*) | 91 |
| **Radish** (*Raphanus sativas longipinratus grp.*) | 75 |
| **Rhubarb** (*Rheum rhabarbarum*) | 74 |
| **Rutabagas** (*Brassica napus var. napobrassica*) | 85 |
| **Salsify** (*Tragopogon porrifolius*) | 87 |
| **Seaweed guso** (*Eucheuma cottonii*) | 100 |
| **Seaweed kawkawayan** (*Gracilaria verrucosa*) | 100 |
| **Seaweed lato** (*Caulerpa recemosa*) | 100 |
| **Sesame leaves** (*Perilla frutescens*) | 100 |
| **Sesbania** (*Sesbania spp.*) | 82 |
| **Shallots** (*Allium ascalonicum*) | 88 |
| **Snap beans** (*Phaseolus vulgaris*) | 92 |
| **Snow peas** (*Pisum sativum*) | 93 |
| **Spinach** (*Spinacia oleracea*) | 67 |
| **Sponge gourd** (*Luffa cylindrica*) | 72 |

# EDIBLE PORTION of SELECTED INGREDIENTS

## CEREALS, TUBERS and VEGETABLES

| FOOD and SCIENTIFIC NAME | PERCENT EDIBLE PORTION |
|---|---|
| **Squash flower** (*Cucurbita spp.*) | 63 |
| **Squash fruit** (*Cucurbita spp.*) | 71 |
| **String bean pods** (*Vigna unguiculata*) | 94 |
| **Sweet potato leaves** (*Ipomoea batatas)* | 50 |
| **Swiss chard** (*Beta vulgaris*) | 92 |
| **Taro leaves** (*Colocasia esculenta*) | 55 |
| **Tomato** (*Solanum lycopersicum*) | 99 |
| **Turnip tuber** (*Brassica rapa Rapifera grp*) | 87 |
| **Turnip greens** (*Brassica rapa Rapifera grp.*) | 70 |
| **Water chestnuts Chinese**, (*Eleocharis dulcis*) | 72 |
| **Water cress** (*Nasturtium officinale*) | 49 |
| **Water spinach/Swamp cabbage** (*Ipomoea aquatica*) | 68 |
| Waxgourd (*Benin casa hispida*) | 74 |
| **Winged bean pods** (*Psophocarpus tetragonolobus*) | 98 |
| **Zucchini** (*Cucurbita spp.*) | 87 |
| **Yambean/Jicama** (*Pachyrhizus spp.*) | 92 |

# EDIBLE PORTION of SELECTED INGREDIENTS

## FRUITS

| FOOD and SCIENTIFIC NAME | PERCENT EDIBLE PORTION |
|---|---|
| **Acerola** (*Malpighia emarginata*) | 80 |
| **Apple** (*Pyrus malus*) | 90 |
| **Apricot** (*Prunus armenjaca*) | 93 |
| **Avocado** (*Persea Americana*) | 72 |
| **Banana bongolan** (*Musa acuminata colla var. suaveoleno*) | 67 |
| **Banana Cavendish** (*Musa acuminata colla var. cavendish*) | 64 |
| **Banana lacatan** (*Musa acuminata colla var. lacatan*) | 69 |
| **Banana latundan** (Musa acuminata colla var. latundan) | 73 |
| **Banana saba** (*Musa acuminata colla var. saba*) | 57 |
| **Bilimbi** (*Averrhoa bilimbi*) | 100 |
| **Blackberry** (*Rubus spp.*) | 96 |
| **Blueberry** (*Vaccinium spp.*) | 95 |
| **Boysenberry** (*Rubus ursinus var. loganobaccus*) | 96 |
| **Breadfruit** (*Artocarpus altilis*) | 75 |
| **Breadnut** (*Artocarpus camansi*) | 70 |
| **Calamansi** (*Citrus microcarpa*) | 38 |

# EDIBLE PORTION of SELECTED INGREDIENTS

## FRUITS

| FOOD and SCIENTIFIC NAME | PERCENT EDIBLE PORTION |
|---|---|
| **Canistel** (*Pouteria campechiana*) | 73 |
| **Carambola** (*Averrhoa carambola*) | 95 |
| **Carissa** (*Carissa macrocarpa*) | 86 |
| **Cherimoya** (*Annona cherimola*) | 69 |
| **Cherry** (*Prunus cerasus/Prunus avium*) | 90 |
| **Coconut meat mature** (*Cocus nucifera*) | 56 |
| **Coconut meat young** (*Cocus nucifera*) | 14 |
| **Coconut sport** (*Cocus nucifera*) | 74 |
| **Cranberry** (*Vaccinium macrocarpon*) | 98 |
| **Custard apple** (*Annona reticulata*) | 57 |
| **Currants black** (*Ribes nigrus*) | 98 |
| **Currants red** (*Ribes rubrum*) | 98 |
| **Dates** (*Phoenix dactylifera*) | 90 |
| **Durian** (*Durio zibethinus*) | 26 |
| **Feijoa** (*Acca sellowiana*) | 57 |
| **Figs** (*Ficus carica*) | 99 |

# EDIBLE PORTION of SELECTED INGREDIENTS

## FRUITS

| FOOD and SCIENTIFIC NAME | PERCENT EDIBLE PORTION |
|---|---|
| **Gooseberry** (*Ribes spp.*) | 100 |
| **Grapefruit** (*Citrus paradise*) | 51 |
| **Guava** (*Psidium guajava*) | 99 |
| **Jackfruit ripe** (*Artocarpus heterophyllus*) | 31 |
| **Java Plum** (*Syzgium cumini*) | 78 |
| **Jujube** (*Ziziphus jujuba*) | 92 |
| **Kiwifruit gold** (*Actinidia chinensis*) | 74 |
| **Kiwifruit green** (*Actinidia deliciosa*) | 77 |
| **Kum quat** (*Fortunella spp.*) | 93 |
| **Lanzon** (*Aglaia domestica*) | 68 |
| **Lemon** (*Citrus limon*) | 52 |
| **Lime** (*Citrus latifolia*) | 59 |
| **Loganberry** (*Robus loganobaccus*) | 94 |
| **Longan** (*Dimocarpus longan*) | 53 |
| **Loquat** (*Eriobotyra japonica*) | 65 |
| **Lipote** (*Syzgium polycephaloides*) | 83 |

# EDIBLE PORTION of SELECTED INGREDIENTS

## FRUITS

| FOOD and SCIENTIFIC NAME | PERCENT EDIBLE PORTION |
|---|---|
| **Lychee/Litchi** (*Litchi chinensis*) | 63 |
| **Mango carabao unripe** (*Mangifera indica*) | 63 |
| **Mango carabao ripe** (*Mangifera indica*) | 69 |
| **Mango indian unripe** (*Mangifera indica*) | 57 |
| **Mango pico ripe** (*Mangifera indica*) | 53 |
| **Mangosteen** (*Garcinia mangostana*) | 26 |
| **Marang** (Artocarpus orodoratissimus) | 29 |
| **Melon cantaloupe** (Cucumis melo) | 57 |
| **Melon honeydew** (Cucumis melo) | 82 |
| **Melon, watermelon** (Citrullus lanatus) | 57 |
| **Nance/Yellow cherries** (Byrsonima crassifolia) | 73 |
| **Nectarine** (Prunus persica var. nucipersica) | 91 |
| **Orange mandarin** (Citrus reticulata) | 74 |
| **Orange ladu** (Citrus lanatus) | 45 |
| **Orange szinkom** (Citrus reticulate) | 46 |
| **Orange Valencia** (Citrus sinensis) | 75 |

# EDIBLE PORTION of SELECTED INGREDIENTS

## FRUITS

| FOOD and SCIENTIFIC NAME | PERCENT EDIBLE PORTION |
|---|---|
| **Papaya ripe** (*Carica papaya*) | 64 |
| **Passion fruit** (*Passiflora edulis*) | 52 |
| **Peach** (*Prunus persica*) | 96 |
| **Pear** (*Pyrus communis*) | 82 |
| **Persimmon** (*Diospyros kaki*) | 84 |
| **Pineapple** (*Ananas comosus*) | 55 |
| **Plum** (*Prunus spp.*) | 94 |
| **Pomegranate** (*Punica granatum*) | 50 |
| **Pomelo** (*Citrus maxima*) | 60 |
| **Rambutan** (*Nephelium lappacum*) | 36 |
| **Raspberry** (*Rubus spp.*) | 96 |
| **Rose apple** (*Syzygium jambos*) | 80 |
| **Roselle** (*Hibiscus sabdariffa*) | 61 |
| **Santol** (*Sandoricum koetjape*) | 59 |
| **Sapodilla** (*Manikara sapota*) | 87 |
| **Sapote** (*Diospyros ebenaster*) | 70 |

# EDIBLE PORTION of SELECTED INGREDIENTS

## FRUITS

| FOOD and SCIENTIFIC NAME | PERCENT EDIBLE PORTION |
|---|---|
| **Soursop** (*Annona muricata*) | 69 |
| **Spanish plum** (*Spondias purpurea*) | 64 |
| **Star apple** (*Chrysophyllium cainito*) | 53 |
| **Strawberry** (*Fragaria vesca*) | 98 |
| **Sugar apple** (*Annona squamosa*) | 55 |
| **Sugar palm** (*Arenga pinnata*) | 100 |
| **Suriname cherry** (*Eugenia uniflora*) | 88 |
| **Tamarind unripe** (*Tamarindus indica*) | 40 |
| **Tamarind ripe** (*Tamarindus indica*) | 40 |
| | |
| | |
| | |
| | |
| | |
| | |

# EDIBLE PORTION of SELECTED INGREDIENTS

## FISH and SHELLFISH

| FOOD and SCIENTIFIC NAME | PERCENT EDIBLE PORTION |
|---|---|
| **Bass striped** (*Morone saxatilis*) | 50 |
| **Carp** (*Cyprinus carpio*) | 55 |
| **Clam freshwater** (*Corbicula manilensis*) | 22 |
| **Clam** (*Pharella spp.*) | 37 |
| **Cod Atlantic** (*Gadus morhua*) | 45 |
| **Cod Pacific** (*Gadus macrocephalus Tilesius*) | 35 |
| **Crab blue** (*Portunus pelagicus*) | 34 |
| **Croaker** (*Micropogonias undulatus*) | 45 |
| **Grouper** (*Epinephelus spp.*) | 49 |
| **Haddock** (*Melanogrammus aeglefinus*) | 45 |
| **Halibut** (*H. Stenolepis Schmidt*) | 60 |
| **Herring big-eyed** (*Illisha hoeveni*) | 31 |
| **Herring deep-bodied** (*Sardinella perforata*) | 59 |
| **Mackerel short-bodied** (*Rastrelliger brachyosomus*) | 52 |
| **Mackerel Spanish** (*Cybium commerson*) | 69 |
| **Mackerel striped** (*Rastrelliger chrysozunus*) | 60 |

# EDIBLE PORTION of SELECTED INGREDIENTS

## FISH and SHELLFISH

| FOOD and SCIENTIFIC NAME | PERCENT EDIBLE PORTION |
|---|---|
| **Milkfish** (*Chanos chanos*) | 65 |
| **Mullet** (*Mugil melinopterus*) | 49 |
| **Mussel** (*Mytillus smaragdinus*) | 56 |
| **Oyster** (*Ostrea spp.*) | 12 |
| **Pompano** (*Apolectus niger*) | 48 |
| **Salmon** (*Elagatis bipinnulatus*) | 44 |
| **Shrimp** (*Penaeus monodon*) | 63 |
| **Snapper** (*Lutjanus malabaricus*) | 44 |
| **Squid** (*Loligo pealli*) | 96 |
| **Tilapia** (*Tilapia mossambica*) | 46 |
| **Trout** (*Salmo* spp.) | 50 |
| **Turbot** (*Psettodes crumei*) | 59 |
| | |
| | |
| | |
| | |

# BIBLIOGRAPHY

Bureau of Agricultural Statistics, Department of Agriculture (n.d.) *Fruit Crops Parameters and Fruiting Season.* Manila, Philippine

Food and Nutrition Research Institute, Department of Science and Technology (1997) *Philippine Food Composition Tables.* Taguig City, Philippines

Food and Nutrition Research Institute, Department of Science and Technology (1994) *Food Exchange List for Meal Planning* 3rd rev. Taguig City, Philippines

Food and Nutrition Section, American Home Economics Association (1993) *Handbook of Food Preparation.* Iowa: Kendall Hunt Publishing Company

Gisslen, W. (2002) *Professional Cooking 6th ed.* New York: John Wiley and Sons

Reyes, G.D., J.P. Siggaoat, S.A. Gruezo, A.V. Lontoc and T.R. Portugal. 1996. *Conversion Factors of Selected Food Items. Phil. J. Nutr.* 18:1-10

U.S. Department of Agriculture, Agricultural Research Service (2014) *USDA National Nutrient Database for Standard Reference Release 27.* Retrieved Dec.1, 2014 from http://www.ars.usda.gov/nutrientdata

U. S. Food and Drug Administration Center for Food Safety and Applied Nutrition Office of Food Labeling (1993) *Guidelines For Determining Metric Equivalents Of Household Measures.* Retrieved December 1, 2005 from http://www.cfsan.fda.gov/~dms/flmetric.html

# INDEX

This page is intentionally left blank.

# About the Authors

**Ma. Christina G. Aquino** is the Executive Director for Planning and Development of the Lyceum of the Philippines University Manila. She is also the LPU Dusit International Project Director, focusing on Tourism and Hospitality Education Programs in the four campuses of LPU and Deputy Quality Management Representative.

She has teaching and administrative work experiences in various academic settings. She was a faculty members of the Department of Hotel Restaurant Institutional Management at the College of Home Economics, University of the Philippines; School Director of Center of Culinary Arts, Manila; and currently, at LPU, a private non-sectarian university. She was formerly the Dean of the College of International Tourism and Hospitality Management from 2006 to 2009. Aside from academic work experiences, she was a flight attendant and a cabin services line instructor for two international airlines, a foodservice provider of an office and educational institution, and a liaison officer of quasi government agency.

Ms. Aquino is the President of Council of Hotel and Restaurant Educators of the Philippines, (COHREP) for two terms, (2011-2012 and 2013-2014), the Associate Board Member for Hotel and Restaurant Association of the Philippines, Vice President (2014-2015) of the Asia Pacific Council of Hotel, Restaurant and Institutional Education, and Secretary of the Tourism Industry Board Foundation Inc., accreditor for Philippine Association of Colleges and Universities Commission on Accreditation, a member of the CHED NCR Regional Quality Assurance Team, a resource person for TESDA in the Tourism sector, and Director of THE-ICE (International Center for Excellence, Tourism and Hospitality Education) an international accrediting agency.

She finished BS HRA (cum laude), MA in Education, major in Educational Administration and completed all the academic requirements of the PhD in Education, specializing in Curriculum Studies, all in the University of the Philippines Diliman Quezon City.

# About the Authors

**Janine P. Siggaoat,** MSc.,R.N.D., received her B.S. in Nutrition in 1991 and M.S. in Applied Nutrition in 1997 from the University of the Philippines Los Baños. She is a board placer in state examination of Nutritionist-Dietitian in the Philippines in 1991. Also, holds a teaching license with a major in the physical sciences.

She teaches undergraduate and graduate nutrition, foods, culinary, chemistry, and health-related courses in different schools and universities in Manila. She was the former School Director of the College of Tourism and Hospitality Management of Central Colleges of the Philippines and the Pacific Global Hospitality Institute. Additionally, she chaired the Nutrition and HRM programs of Manila Tytana Colleges.

Before joining the academe, she worked as the Senior Researcher at the Nutrition Center of the Philippines. A Research Specialist II at the Food and Nutrition Research Institute of the Department of Science and Technology. She started working as a Research Associate at the Department of Agricultural Extension and Rural Studies, University of the Philippines Los Baños on finishing her undergraduate study.

With her years of experience in teaching and research, her passion to learn further and share her craft, she is now into book writing. She also devotes time into private consulting and training.

Made in the USA
Coppell, TX
12 March 2023